The Young & the Elevated

This book is dedicated to Darrell Goins

May your soul rest easy.

The Young & the Elevated
G.P.B.

Prologue

It was December tenth. It was not the coldest of winters ever, but it was cold enough. Only the crackheads along with the fearless who dared to accommodate them with their habits, would risk their own lives being outside.

As Dee, Will and Man cut their way back into the alley they never paid any attention to the two guys that were lingering behind Wills car.

"I hope you ain't scared to fuck Tee-Tee's friend tonight." Will teased Man.

"Naw man, I ain't scared. She always be faking everything whenever she is in front of ya'll, but behind closed doors she's not ready."

Dee had been joking and laughing along with his boyz, but all the while he had an eerie feeling in the pit of his gut that something just wasn't quite right. It was a bit too quiet. Before his being able to say anything about it to them, two guys in all black attire raised up with loaded Glocks.

"What's up now fuckers?" One of the two guys shouted boisterously at them.

As Dee quickly reached towards his waist for his 357 Magnum, he had forgotten he had left it back in the trap because the *Jump Outs (cops)* were out lurking. As all three men turned running for their lives multiple gunshots went off sounding as if fireworks were booming on the fourth of July. *Boom…pow… pow… bang bang…*I'm hit! Man yelled out to Dee who was running ahead of him. Dee stopped immediately in his tracks. He turned looking back over his shoulder and seeing that his right hand man had been seriously hurt. While bullets continued flying passed their heads, Dee knew he needed to react quickly getting over to Man and moving him away from the danger. Dee searched the area looking around for Will, but he did not see him in sight. He wondered if he had made his way to safety. After things had quieted down and he had moved Man away to a much safer place to hide. Dee ran back towards his vehicle noticing fresh drops of blood on the ground. He knew that this could not be a good sign. As he followed the trail of blood it led him to where he found Will, who had been wounded. He had been shot twice in his back, one time in his leg, and once to his face. "Oh shit." Dee placed his hand covering his mouth as he knelt at his friend's side where he laid in a pool of blood. Dee again had to think quickly as he witnessed the dangers of his friends' possibility of losing his life as he was gasping for air. He could not fathom him dying in front of him much less in his arms. Dee immediately stood up from his position then bending over he picked up Will's limp body into his arms before his running to his car carrying dead weight. He opened the door placing Will's limp body inside as gently as he could resting it against the back seat. Dee took out his cellphone while hastily moving around the car to get into the driver's seat where he made a call to his other homies instructing them to come and get Man, who he had no other option, but to leave behind in *the Dip.* Driving as fast as a bat would out of hell, Dee, swerving the car made a sharp left turn before his speeding down Florida Avenue. He pressed the gas pedal to the floor not stopping for any red lights along the way. Suddenly, from out of nowhere with the force and impact of a fast moving train, a silver truck smashed the driver side of Dee's BMW 745iL.

"Oh my God…somebody help! Please call for the ambulance!" Bystanders were yelling.

As Dee's head laid pressed against the steering wheel he went in and out of consciousness. All his thoughts were about was how they could have allowed themselves to get caught slipping like that in the first place, and about who would pay? *Who were those guys? I hope I make it out alive because payback is one of hell a bitch.* Dee knew money always talked and the G.P.B. carried more than enough to make a *thirsty rat* say cheese on a Thanksgiving Thursday. Dee could faintly hear surrounding voices asking if he were okay, along with the sounds of sirens in the background. He listened for Will's voice calling out his name just before his losing consciousness.

Chapter One – Eight years earlier

It was in the middle of spring as Dee sat in class thinking about the next upcoming basketball game. He was a star basketball player for Lincoln Knights. He had every school in the District of Columbia wanting him to come and play ball for them. Weighing in at six three one-hundred and seventy pounds, he did it all. Some people had said he played the game as good as John Wall, but with more of a quickness and ups. In his last game he had dunked on a six foot six forward and had the crowd going crazy.

When the bell rang for school to end Dee was sitting deep in thought and had no idea class was over until man pushed him out his chair telling him to snap out of it. Man and Dee were the best of friends and they went back like flats on four tires. They met when they were each five years old and you could not tell either of them that they were not brothers by their blood. They both had grown up in the very same neighborhood as well as living in the same apartment building. Man who was five foot nine, one hundred-seventy-five pounds and he enjoyed boxing in his spare time. Growing up, the kids in the neighborhood were afraid of Man and not much had changed as he grew older. He thought he was such a pretty boy with swagger, but dared people to jump stupid. I remember when he was in the sixth grade and he had smacked the gym teacher with his peanut butter and jelly sandwich. Mr. Gray tried his best to snatch him up, but Man was too quick by side-stepping Mr. Gray before his hitting him with a three piece that sat him down on his ass looking quite stupid while all the kids laughed. Rumors were told around school he had chosen to leave teaching after that incident occurred. Because Man had never lost a fight before, he was always being compared to Floyd Mayweather, because he also had never lost a fight regardless of his size, speed, or due to the strength the other person had.

"Why was you dazed out like that in class?" Man asked Dee while they were walking over to the corner store.

"I don't know. Sometimes I just think about my future and what lies ahead of me."

"Okay cool." Man said giving him that look of concern. "Just don't lose your mind 'cause you know bullshit ain't nothing."

"Let me get some sheets and a box of Mike and Ikes. Don't forget the two ice teas." Man said to Dee as he opened the refrigerator.

After leaving the store they began walking along the street when they heard their names being called.

"Aye! Dee, Man hold on. Wait."

They both looked around to see Will getting off the metro bus coming from school. Will was a kid from the hood who was quiet, and smart as hell. If you asked him anything about math, spelling, history...etc., he would always know the answer. And if he didn't you could bet he would find it as soon as possible. Will was a guy who was five foot seven, one hundred and sixty-five pounds who had the look of intelligence all the ladies seemed to love. They compared his looks to that of Juelz Santana the well-known rapper. Will was the one who began wearing the fitted-clothing and the latest pairs of snapbacks before niggas even thought about it. And that's real talk.

"I got some Kush. Let's match something up." Will said grabbing a pack.

Dee and Man both looked at each other saying the same thing. "Bet that."

When they made it around the way they walked straight to the neighborhood Rec center.

"Aye, Will roll up. We going to be over on the court waiting for you." Dee tossed him the *Loud marijuana* and sheets he had.

When they showed up to the court everybody along with their momma's was there from old ball players to kids, as they watched a good five on five game go down.

"Aye Dee…you running next with us?" Moe along with some of his homies asked.

"Maybe later ya'll. I got some shit I got to do. But I'll catch ya'll later."

Dee and Man walked across to the playground where they saw Will.

"Got damn! This sheet is as wet as shit." Man said as he used the lighter to dry it a little.

"You always complaining when I roll up nigga. Damn! Can't you just please cut a nigga some slack?" Will asked shaking his head.

Man lit the jay before his taking two hard pulls from it before his passing it. "Damn this some fire."

"Everything is fire to you." Dee said as they all laughed.

"Nigga fuck you. You know how I stay with that pressure." He nudged Dee.

Will's phone started ringing. *I'ma hustla. Ima-Ima hustla.* "Hello?"

"Heyyy…Will. This Niesha."

"Oh yeah. What's up boo?"

"I'm cooling. What you doing?" She placed the hoop earring through the hole in her ear.

"I'm hanging with my homies at the Rec on the playground. Why…what's up?"

"Why? Boy-Please! Me, and my girls coming down there so you better be there." She hung up.

Niesha was one of those girls that really had the beauty, but did not have much when it came to having brains. She had the sexiest lips with a brick house body. Five feet five, one hundred-thirty-five pounds with a sweet ass like a peach with the gorgeous face of Nia Long. She was a trouble maker, but could backup whatever she brought. She was also madly in love with Will and would do anything that man said to do.

"Them Clifton Street bitches are coming down here so don't ya'll leave me." Will said.

"Cool. Let's hit the court then." Dee said as he stood up with them following. Feeling higher than a kite and relaxed, they all walked onto the basketball court side by side ready to play the b-ball game. They got on the court at the right time because Moe stole the ball and made the game winning lay-up.

"Game time!" Moe screamed as he tossed the ball into the air.

"Who got next?" They all asked.

"We do." Man said as he picked up two of the losers from the previous game with the three of us ready to play.

They went up ten to six. Moe was on fire. Will was not keeping up with Moe's offense. Man had become angry that Will was playing soft on defense, so he began checking Moe himself. I went into overdrive as I blocked the ball, came down court and hit a three pointer.

"Let's go." I yelled to my team because I hated losing.

Niesha and some of her friends came right on time because Will stole the ball making a lay-up trying to look as if he had done something. We went back and forth for a while. The score was now fifteen to fourteen and we were losing the game on the wall. I knew I had to do something, so I quickly drove to the left, crossed over to the right pulling a three. As the ball left my hands I thought I was going to miss the basket, but to my surprise it went in and we won the game. We all gave each other *dap* saying good game as we left off the court.

"That was a close one today Dee." Will said as he gave me *dap*.

"Yeah. If I had not switched up on the defense we would have lost." Man said pushing Will to the side laughing before we all joined in.

"Let's go get something to eat with Niesha and them after we change." Will said.

"Okay. Cool." They all agreed going into the locker room to change into different clothing.

"That was a good game ya'll. Niesha and her group of friends said as they walked up.

"Thanks to your *"Pooh Butt,"* we almost lost." Man said.

"Shut up Man! You always saying something negative about my Boo." Niesha hit Man on his arm.

"Stop playing girl." Man said.

"Before I forget my manners let me introduce China and Asia, my home-girls. These guys here are Will's buddies, Dee and Man."

"Nice to meet ya'll." Both of the girls said almost in unison.

They all shook hands.

It was as if I could not help myself. I looked at China with lust in my eyes because she was a bad bitch. She did not at all look like the type of girl that would hang around Niesha. But then again who was I to judge. Will did not look like the type to hang with us either.

"Ya'll ladies hungry?" Man asked waiting for a response.

"It don't matter." Niesha said as they all walked together to the Popeye's.

"Yo… Dee spark that jay back up before we get something to eat." Will said.

"Okay, cool. Give me my lighter… Man."

"Do ya'll ladies smoke? And I am not talking to you Neisha." Dee said laughing.

China and Asia both responded, "Sometimes."

When Dee sparked the jay up, he had tapped it a couple times before he passed it to China. She looked around before taking two soft pulls. She coughed a couple of times before passing it on. When they arrived at the Popeye's everybody placed their orders. Dee paid for China's and his meal to show her that he was really interested in getting to know her more. Before they parted ways Dee gave China his number telling her to give him a call because he wanted to talk with her. She had not given him any clue that she was feeling him too. Over the next month, China and Dee became closer as they learned they had a lot in common with each other. They talked on the phone every night and spent lots of free time together. China was two years older than Dee but it did not feel that way to her because he was mature and built for his age. She took the time to attend his games cheering him on. They also went to the library helping each other study. He had also asked her to the prom, but she decided to play big by telling him she would think about it, all the while knowing that she wanted to be on his arm because they looked good together.

Chapter Two

Ring Ring Ring.

"You have a pre-paid call from the Petersburg Federal Detention Center. Please press one to accept the call."

"Whatz up lil cuz? I been hearing good things about you breaking school records." Fiz said.

"Cut it out Big Cuz. I'm just playing my game, but you know how it is."

"Yeah I do. I just wanted to wish you good luck on the last game. Play hard because I know that you got a ship coming your way."

"Yeah okay Cuz. I feel you. I will play this one for you Big Cuz." Dee told him before hanging up.

There were two days left before the game. Dee focused solely on his game plan and strategies against his opponent. The team they would be playing against was sixteen and zero and could go down in history as the team to be undefeated in the last twenty years. Their star player whose name was Tay was a six foot six two-hundred pound small forward. He ran the court as if he were an NBA star. Dee sat in his room watching tapes of the games. He noticed eighty percent of their points came from Tay. Dee was not going to allow that to happen.

Game time

It was the last game. There was twenty minutes left until the game would start. Everybody was there from KDP to KDY niggas. 1-7 Boys was there to cheer their favorite pick, Dee on for the victory. The crowd was live and the bleachers were packed. Many of the hood legends were in attendance such as, *CUT crew, 1-4 Zone*, the *640 Naughty Boys and etcetera.* Dee scanned through the crowd finding his homies, Will and Man sitting with their girls. Will and Man gave Dee that, *go for what you know* nod, and that was all he needed.

It was in the fourth quarter. Dee's team was up by three points, one minute-forty-two seconds left. Tay was having his way and went up for a lay-up. Dee came in from the side blocking the ball. The crowd was going wild. Dee had a fast break slamming the ball into the basket so hard he thought the rim had been broken. When he came down, Tay elbowed him hard in the face. Man jumped up from where he was sitting in the bleachers, running onto the court punching Tay in his face with such force, it knocked him dizzy. CUT crew ran onto the court backing up their man Tay, while the 1-7 Boys jumped in to help Dee and Man. An all-out brawl then went down leaving people both injured and hurt. When the *Twelve* soon arrived people scattered from the gymnasium floor like both rats and roaches. Dee searched through the crowd before his eyes caught sight of Niesha, China, and Will running together towards the spot where they met up every day afterschool.

"What the fuck just happened?" Dee asked still feeling dizzy from the elbow he had just taken to the face. "Where the hell is Man at?"

"I saw Man leave with Moe." Will said as they walked down the street.

Just as they were crossing 16th and Fuller Street, a black Lexus slowly pulled up beside them with a group of dudes inside it?

"*Whadd-up* Dee? Let them 1-7 niggas know it's *on and poppin'* now for pulling a move like that at the game."

Dee did not say anything. He just mugged on them and kept walking with Will and the girls. Before the Lexus pulled away the driver leaned out the window of the car firing a couple shots out of his loaded gun into the air. *Boom, boom, boom!* Dee along with the others ducked to find safety. The car turned moving away from them as it sped recklessly down the street. *Scrrrr…*

They all walked quietly together along the street dropping the girls off in front of their home on, 14th and Columbia Road NW.

"Dee don't you do anything stupid." China said while looking him in the eyes.

"I will try my best, but if those niggas say some shit to me again like that we going to take it to the streets."

But what he really wanted to tell her was he did not give a fuck. Since they played with him he was going to do what his Cuzin Fiz taught him years ago before he got locked up. Which was to *bust a nigga's ass with that chopper.* He pulled China in closer to him. She took him by surprise with her giving him a passionate kiss that seemed to last for hours. Will and Niesha who were surprised just as well laughed at them. After what seemed an eternity to both Niesha and Will they had to tell them that it was enough and it was time for them to part ways. Dee knew where his heart was and he was ready to move to third base with China, home running her ass as if it were the end of a baseball game in the ninth inning.

When Dee went inside his building all he could smell was the *Purp* that was lingering in the air. He knew exactly where the familiar aroma was coming from. He jetted down the stairs leading to the basement where everyone from the hood enjoyed just hanging out and chilling at night. People were sitting around smoking, drinking, and shooting dice. When they had spotted Dee coming through the doors they all showed love giving him dap while cheering him on about the good game he had played. When he spotted Man they gave one another that brotherly hug they always shared. Not having a care in the world, Dee sat down on a chair before grabbing Tia, one of the twins, pulling her down onto his lap flirting with her while he hit jay after jay in rotation. Dee knew how far he could go with her and he surely was going to try his hand at it.

"Let's go to the laundry mat." Dee whispered as the weed began to kick in.

They stood from the chair with her leading him by the hand into the room next door. Once they were alone together in the room he locked the door behind them before he began kissing on her neck. She moaned softly. He undid the top button of her pants before his pulling her shirt up over her head. She grabbed his manhood surprised at how large his manhood was. His penis stood at attention ready to put in the work. Turning her around then bending her over he, stuck his nine inch python gently into her love box.

"*Damn, fuck -shit*! Keep going."

She moaned as Dee stroked her hard and fast with sweat dripping off their bodies. Before his having to nut he stopped for a moment leading her to a chair that was sitting in the corner of the room. He sat down allowing her to climb on top of his manhood before her riding him slow. He felt as though he was in Heaven. While focusing mainly on his eyes,she looked at him closely. There was something within them that willed her body to move as if they were intertwined in a slow dance together. He gripped her hips raising her body up then down picking up speed as sweat formed on their foreheads.

"I'm about to come!" She screamed.

Dee held onto her tightly as they both climaxed while trying to catch their breaths.

"Damn girl." Dee gave her a slight smile.

Tia responded back with a smile of happiness knowing that she had satisfied him. They both adjusted their clothing before going back into the other room joining the others. On the way out the door Dee playfully slapped Tia on her behind with the palm of his hand. She looked over her shoulder smiling at him. They returned to the other room to find Man along with Tia's twin sister Kia, still there waiting for them.

"What was ya'll doing in the laundry mat?" Kia asked being nosey.

"Just talking." Tia replied while looking at Dee to collaborate her lie.

They smoked one more jay before them parting ways. When Dee had arrived home everybody was asleep. After his taking a quick shower he prepared himself for bed. He turned the light on the lamp beside his bed off before he said a small prayer while sitting in the dark.

"God thank-you for keeping me and my loved ones safe. I want to thank you for letting me live to see another day. Please bless everybody even the killers, thugs and drug dealers. God Bless." Crawling across the covers on his bed he passed out.

Chapter Three

Things were back to normal as the weeks went by. Man had gotten suspended for the rest of the school year, but I persuaded the principal into letting him go to the prom and to graduate with our class. China finally gave in to the idea of going with me by accepting my invitation to the prom. I still did not get the *cookies* from her, but I knew that time would come soon enough for me. I was still hitting both the twin's freaky asses anyway, so I was not about to trip.. It was rumored after the basketball brawl Tay had begun the unsavory task of robbing people. He must have robbed the wrong person because a month later I heard he was found in the alley off of Fairmont Street with two bullets in his head. Shame all that talent had gone to waste. When Prom night had arrived, me and my boys we were all looking sharp. I wore a pair of Giorgio Armani slacks, along with my Montcler button down tailored shirt. I sported a pair of Steve Madden kicks to jump off my look. As a compliment I also wore a pair of gold studs. Thanks went out to my father who had sent me the money for the prom and to my Cuzin Fiz for taking me out when he had come home. China wore a short black Gucci dress that her mom had given her. It was beautiful and it fitted her body perfectly allowing me to see her every curve. She wore a pair of Gucci heels which matched her ensemble. With her topping it all off she carried a green clutch in her hand. She looked so stunning I had almost forgotten that she was my date for a moment. Will and Man both went without dates, but they still dressed for the occasion. They each had on their feet a pair of Prada kicks and a of Armani Exchange slacks. Will had dressed in a red and black Nautica shirt, while Man had chosen to wear a black Polo shirt. We were all dressed to impress. We hopped in the limo making our way over to the prom. Will was not a student at our school so it did not bother him when he decided to sneak in two bottles of Moet through the back door. As the night went on Man, myself, and a few others of the team mates drank champagne while we laughed and talked a lot of shit. Will did not drink, so he was not tripping in the manner in which we were. When the slow music began playing over the sound system, I reached out my hand to China asking her to come dance with me. We held one another closely for what seemed to be for an eternity. She rested her head onto my shoulder.

"I think I am ready." She whispered.

I didn't understand what she meant by that at the time, but I would when the night was over.

The prom was about to end and I was tipsy. We were all feeling good and we were ready to leave. We all collected our belongings making our way over to the exit doors.

"About damn time!" Will scoffed.

We all laughed at him knowing that what he had said meant he was ready to get his smoke on. As soon as we all climbed back into the Limo, I rolled two fat *Backwoods* jays. Sitting in the back of the Limo we talked and laughed about how the night had gone.

"I'm drunk as shit." Man took two more pulls off the Backwoods.

"I bet you is… *Weed hoover.*" Will said as we all cracked up laughing.

We rode around the town for a good hour in the Limo before it was time for the driver to drop us off again. When China, and I walked quietly into my house everyone was fast asleep. We went into my room. I locked my door so that we could have some privacy. We both undressed. For the first time I was feeling nervous around China. Her nipples were hard, and I did not know what else to do, so I just looked at them. We stood together quietly naked until I kissed her lips softly breaking the ice. I wanted my having sex to be different this time. I kissed her neck, then both of her breasts until her breathing increased rapidly. Moving my hands slowly downward so I could remove her panties away from her *Valley*, I was surprised to see that she had neatly shaven her *coochie spot*. Something I had only seen previously in porno movies. I sucked lightly on her pussy lips sticking my tongue in and out of her hole. Even though this was my first time ever eating pussy, I felt as though I did know what I was doing. She didn't complain, so that said a lot to me. I came up for air taking a minute to grab the condom from my pocket, which I kept to have safe sex. I pulled it on my penis and I entered her. For the first time in my fourteen years it felt right having sex. An hour had passed while we continued to make love before her falling asleep in my arms. I held her as tightly as I could without my waking her. I did not want to ever let her go. The next morning I would receive a call from my father that would shock me.

Chapter four

My summer was getting off to a very good start. I finally had sex with China, my Cuzin Fiz came home, and my dad and I finally had a man to man talk. I can still remember when my dad had been the King of drugs. His name was Dennis then, and we were all living the high-life. We lived in a nice condo off of Connecticut Avenue. He had some of the nicest friends, and you could always find him driving a money green Jaguar, or either a sky blue Benz. He would always buy for me the lastest toys and games. The only thing he asked was for me to stay in school to continue with my education. I still remember the conversations we had from way back then, as if it were yesterday.

"Dee when you grow up you need an education, or you won't survive in this world. If you do not learn math skills how are you going to count your money?"

It was always Dee this, Dee that. At the time, I did not want to hear any of that shit, but when I grew up becoming older I began to understand what he had meant.

My growing up began very quickly on May 17, 1988 very quickly. My classes had ended for the day and I was waiting outside for my dad because he was the one who would normally pick me up. I waited and I waited, but he never showed up. I walked back inside the school building before I began blowing up his phone. *Ring…ring…ring…*

I repeatedly called him over and over again, but he never answered. This was unlike him, so I did what I thought would be best by walking home alone. When I arrived to my dad's condo I seen it all.

"Aye Dennis. The police are surrounding your condo." One of the white guys told him that hung around with my dad.

"It is eight motherfuckers in this room and one of you bitches set me up!" My dad said yelling with fire in his eyes.

He reached his hand beneath the bottom of the couch grabbing the Mac he had hidden there. He pointed the strap at each of the people before his telling them to strip down. While he was waiting for this one guy with the light blue eyes to strip down, the DC police came and kicked in his door with force. *Boom…boom…boom…*

"Everybody get down!"

By the time they had finished with raiding my Pop's spot the police had discovered about fifty pounds of HyDro, 3,000 E pills, 3 keys of Coke, a

Mac II and a large stash of bills inside the mattress. This was the District of Columbia's largest raid since the R. Edmond case. My dad was able to make his bond two days later. After his leaving the country having used a fictitious name on his passport, not a single soul has ever laid eyes on him since. Every once in a while a couple of FBI agents stop by knocking on my grandmother's door asking questions as if they believed they were going to get any answers. They had even offered me money to tell them where he was. My answers always remained the same.

"I told you before that I don't know. I have not spoken with him. I also keep telling ya'll he is not my father." I would laugh.

I just hope that when I do get the chance to see my father again, he will know that I have been loyal to him and that family makes us related, but loyalty makes us blood. When everything was in the clear I climbed out of the hole that was under the staircase. I saw some yellow tape crossing the door for no one to enter as I was walking up the stairs that led to my dad's condo. I ignored the warning tape placing my hand on the knob and turning it. When the door opened I could see all the mess inside. Walking towards the kitchen and to the refrigerator I opened the freezer pulling all the boxes out of it. The police must not have been hard enough because I found two thousand dollars in the frozen string bean box, and the remainder of my dad's both heavy and expensive jewelry as well. After my placing the merchandise into my crayon box, I called my cousin telling him where he could find me. After my telling Fiz what happened over at my dad's condo I gave him a portion of the money keeping the other half for myself.

By the end of the summer season in 2001, I had turned fourteen years old, and around the way things began to heat up. Uptown was *turnt'* up and the beef between 1-7 Boys and Cut Crew became real. A couple of my homies had gotten hit up in the crossfire, so we just clapped back hitting them where it hurt. Every day it seemed as if the Cut Crew was shooting at niggas in the mall every time they crossed paths with their *Opps.* On the upside of things I had finally made a selection of the school I would attend in the fall, but on the downside China and I were no longer chilling together. Will, Man and I were walking through the alley. We were on our way to my apartment building when from the corner of my eye, I spotted a white rock inside a bag that was the size of a mini football.

"Aye ya'll! What in the fuck is this?" I stooped down picking it up."

"I don't know what that is, but I have seen my brothers cook that shit up before." Will said.

Man laughed. "It's crack stupid. Ya'll need to pay attention to watching New Jack City."

Picking up the white rock I tucked it far down inside my hoodie as we continued walking on. When we were inside my room I pulled it out. Grabbing my cousin's scale from the back of the closet I weighed it. 82.3 grams.

"We rich!" Will's face looked as serious as if he was having a heart attack.

I grabbed us some hood movies and we sat for hours watching Belly, Menace to Society, New Jack City, Cocaine Cowboys and Paid in Full. After we watched the movies we began to feel as though we were fully educated with a degree in weighing, cooking and the distribution of Crack Cocaine. When we went back outside our eyes were wide open to the new world that had been introduced by the movies we had just watched. Now that we understood what was going on we were ready to make sure it was our time to get money. We sat on the corner where everybody hung out as we watched paying close attention to anything and everything moving. We even wrote our cell numbers down on pieces of paper, so that when we saw crackheads we could tell them to give us a call. The next day we did everything we had seen in the movies we had watched. I began cutting the rock down in blocks, Man bagged it and, Will weighed it. When we finished working we went down to the Rec. where we knew drugs weren't being sold. We spoke with Jimmy who was the neighborhood crackhead. We gave him a twenty rock telling him we had more of where that came from for sale. Twenty minutes later, like crazy our cellphones were blowing up with numbers from all over. Whoever we spoke with we always kept it short telling them to meet us behind the Rec. It was not before long that we had pockets full of money with no more crack, and with nobody to supply us. I suggested an idea to my boys and they went with it because we did not want to get played, or to have anyone work us for our money.

"What the hell are we going to do now?" Man asked.

"Buy some more crack." Will said.

I was silent because I had to think.

"Just like that? And who do we suppose to get it from?" Man asked getting frustrated.

They both went back and forth as if they were in a tennis match until an idea hit me.

"Let's spend half on some weed. Sell the weed, and while we are waiting look for the best price and we need to find someone we can trust. We still should have a little money coming in from the weed sells."

They both looked at me with smiles widening across their faces. I instantly knew they were down with it. Then From out of nowhere Will made a statement.

"We need a gun too."

"For what Will?" Man asked.

I just looked at both of them shaking my head.

"Because. Remember in the movie Paid in Full he got shot and he got robbed. If he had carried a gun with him they would have thought twice about fucking with him."

We all agreed that Will did make a lot of sense.

Chapter Five

To my surprise the plan I came up with actually worked out great for us. Will sold a lot more weed than we did, but it didn't matter because all the money we made went to the same stash spot anyway. It was the middle of summer and we still did not find anyone we wanted to deal with, so we just kept selling *Loud* just to keep the money rolling in. I was getting dressed and ready to hit the block when Man busted in my room with *G* the neighborhood thief.

"Got damn Man! You can't knock nigga? You act like this your crib, *Scrap*' I joked.

We dapped before our sitting down.

"*G* got a dog to sell." Man said cutting his joke short.

When I looked at *G* he pulled two straps out. A 9mm Ruger and a 32 Special and a box of 9mm bullets. He laid it all out on my bed.

"What you want for '*em?*" I asked picking up the 9mm up from my bed examining it.

"200 Nifty." *G* said looking like he came up.

I looked at Man first then at *G* in the eyes and told him *"Hell no!"* just to test his guts. I knew he had snaked a nigga out for them and I was not taking a risk on spending that much money on hot guns. He had me fucked up.

"Aw'right *G*, you already know… that I know how you got these joints. It might got bodies and some more shit on them. So this is what I will do. I will give you Two-hundred Seventy-five for all of this shit here, and if not… I'll take the 9mm… ruff you and make Man knock you out." I said as I gave him a cold stare.

He must have become scared because when he looked at Man he said… "Cool."

I gave him the two-hundred seventy-five dollars and we chilled for about a minute. I made sure I had mentioned to *G* about coming up in the drug game with us telling him that when he was ready we could take over. He nodded his head. When we were leaving out of the building, heading to go down on the block he told me he would think about getting down with us.

Will

I kept asking my brother Fatz about that *White Girl Cocaine,* but he kept taking me as a joke. I pulled out a couple stacks of money.

"What the hell you doing with all that money?" Fatz asked.

Fatz sat thinking about everything I had said for a minute. I knew that he was beginning to see the same of what we saw. Dollar signs. His eyes told everything.

"Look here Lil Will. I really don't want to do it, but I know that you and your boys going to do what you'll want to…so I guess that it is best I look out for you'll."

It shocked me when he said 850.00 an ounce. I almost fainted when he said that. I called Dee immediately telling him the good news.

"Where you at Dee?"

"I'm at the block party with man. Why what's up?" Dee asked.

"I got some great news. Stay there. I'm on my way." Will said before hanging up.

Giving my brother a hug good-bye, I told him I would call him when I was ready. I literally ran out of the door to anxiously meet up with Dee. The block was packed like a college campus party and I could smell nothing but some trouble. I spotted Man and he was talking to Kia. I quickly made my way over to him.

"What's up ya'll?"

I gave Kia a hug and gave Man some dap.

"Where Dee at?" Will asked.

"He's standing over there." Man said pointing towards Dee, Fiz, and Moe standing together in a semi-circle.

Dee

When we got on the block everybody was there from the Pussy pound to Most Wanted. They showed love like always. I pulled Moe and Fiz to the side letting them know I needed to talk about something. They seemed to be cool with it and joined in.

"Who ya'll know that got that Paris Hilton?" I asked looking for some coke.

They both looked as if I was joking before they both burst into laughter.

"You have got to be joking like shit Cuz!" Fiz said still laughing.

"I'm serious." I said with a straight face.

"I will see about asking my peoples." Moe said after seeing the seriousness in my face.

My phone started ringing. It was Will calling.

"Hold on a minute ya'll." I said speaking to Moe and Fiz as I answered my phone.

"Okay Will. Meet me on the block." I hang up.

We all made small talk for a little while before I saw Will walking my way.

Man

When I had bumped into *G* and he told me he was selling straps I knew step one of our plans to sell drugs was done. When we went to Dee's house and he said that he negotiated a great price I knew things were about to take off, but I did not know where we were going to get the coke from? When we made it to the block party I ran into Kia and kicked the BOBO with her for a few minutes before Will's walking up from out of nowhere. Before I knew it Dee, Will and I were leaving the block making our way over to the basement of the apartment building.

"Dee *roll up*." Man said as he threw the bag of Kush at him.

"Before we begin talking about the good news let's smoke first." Will said smiling.

Dee sparked the Jay taking three soft pulls off of it before passing it along over to Man. Then he proceeded to roll a second jay.

"My brother told me he will give us ounces for the 850." Will said feeling his high.

"Got Damn!" Man said as he started coughing before his sitting up straight.

"Now we have to find out if it's any good." Dee said.

"Well, ain't but one way for us to find out." Will agreed

"We now have those guns to protect us too." Man added.

"Oh yea...Where they at then? Will asked not believing them whole heartedly.

"They in my shoebox where the money's at. It's a 9mm and a 32 special." Dee said.

"Oh shit nigga! Do they work? Did you'll bust 'dem joints off yet?" Will asked.

"Nah, not yet Will. We just got ahold of them joints today." Man handed him the box with the 32 Special.

Will looked the 32 over before his replacing it back inside the box.

"Okay cool. Let's get out of here." Will said.

They all agreed. They were headed back to the block party when they heard a ring of shots fire off. *Boom…boom…boom!* People were running and screaming for help in all directions. We ran back to the building to chill until all the chaos had died down. When things quieted we went back down onto the block where Moe told us the story about everything.

"Some niggas that were in a black Lexus drove passed and just started firing off. Fiz got hit and Domo was grazed in the leg. I ain't sure if they okay." Moe said.

Before Moe could even finish speaking his words I knew it was time for us to find out if those guns we had worked for sure. I looked over at Man. He could clearly see what was going on in my mind. *Retaliation.* We split up for a minute to prepare ourselves for what had to go down. When night fell I put on my black sweat pants, matching black hoodie along with a pair of my black Nike shoes. I checked the 9mm to make sure the safety was off. I stretched out across my bed and I waited.

Man drifted off to sleep, but when he heard the loud knocking at his window it made him jump reaching for the 32 special he had placed on his dresser. He placed his finger on the trigger ready to pull and to discharge when he heard his name being called. His heart muscles relaxed when he realized it was only Will letting him know it was time for them to go and take care of business. On his way outside, Man saw Dee coming down the back fire escape.

Will had borrowed the car from his brother to drop them off on top of the hill.

"Make sure you meet us down the hill near the alley. Keep the car running with the lights off. Man told Will just before he pulled away from the curb.

"Dee, you see those niggas over there in front of that house?" Man asked.

"Yeah bro." I said taking in a few deep breaths.

"That's our Vicks." Man said after his handing me a pair of gloves.

For the very first time in my life I felt fear in my heart. For a quick second my past fourteen years flashed so fast forward I couldn't believe it. I felt my hands getting sweaty while I prayed to God these guns we held worked. My anxiety left for a minute and before I knew it, I raised my gun and had begun *clapping* as I ran down on them niggas. *Boom..! Boom…! Boom!*

I was looking down on them niggas who were both stuck and stunned, as blood oozed out of their bodies.

"Come on Dee! Come on!" I heard Man saying as he pulled my arm snapping me out of it. I ran fast down the alley to the street where Will was parked.

"Go! Go! Go!" We both yelled at Will.

After it was over and I made it home that night I could not believe what me, and my boys had done. I prayed it was the right thing for us to do. I tossed, while turning in my sleep dreaming of dead bodies lying on the concrete all night. *No! No! No stop*! I screamed out loud as my dream seemed so real. I woke up to my grandmother's voice. She was shaking me telling me to get up. My body was drenched in my sweat soiling the linens on my bed.

"It's okay now son." My grandmother held me tightly not caring if I were sweaty or not.

"Thanks grandma. I guess I was having a bad dream and I couldn't wake up."

"The devil was riding your back baby. He did not want you to wake up. He wanted you to suffer." She said while still holding me. "You just need to keep praying. How about I go and fix you a good breakfast? That will make you feel better." She kissed me again before she left my room.

I looked at my phone. 6:25pm. I had missed a few calls from China, Tia and surprisingly from my mother. I had not spoken with China in awhile, so I made myself a mental note about spending some time with her because things were going to become very hectic once school was to begin in a few weeks. I returned China's call that morning and we did have a lot to talk about. She told me how much she had missed me being with me, and asked questions about the shooting she heard had happened the previous night. She also told me I was the only thing she had been thinking about.

It had gotten hot on the block after the shooting and *Fifty,* the District of Columbia police, sat on the block stopping everyone from getting there grind on. It was a ghost town. I knew we had to move fast getting the Rec back to popping as soon as possible before the police began clearing the streets getting things back to normal.

Ring... ring... ring...

"Aye Will this Dee. Wake your ass up."

I was tired as hell, but I sat up and talked to my Homie.

"I am up now Dee. What's good?"

"Tell Fatz to give us four of them girls. I'll buy two of them. You and Man can buy the other two."

"Okay Dee, I'm on it now."

I finished eating the breakfast my grandmother prepared for me before hopping into the shower. I quickly dressed so that I could meet the boys down at the Rec.

When I arrived on the scene it was already live on the b-ball court. I met up with Will and Man.

"Fatz only had three of them thangs left." Will said.

"I'm cool with that." Dee gave Will his half of the money.

"Man… you call Jimmy so that we can cut up." Dee told him.

Man

I took out my phone calling Jimmy. He did not answer, but I knew he was somewhere around. Leaving him a text. I waited. Ten minutes later he had dialed my phone back asking me *"what's up."* I got straight to it telling him we needed his spot. He was down with us using his place. He knew he was going to receive a couple of rocks anyway.

When we arrived he had a female chilling with him. He handed us the keys with his leaving out the house without any problems, nor questions. We got straight down to business with washing our hands and putting gloves on. I weighed it. 84 grams. Will got the razors and plates ready while Dee threw the 12/12 bags on the table. After endless hours of putting in work we were done.

"Damn I'm tired as shit. Where is the tree at?" Dee said walking to the bathroom.

"I already got two jays rolled up. Let me wash my hands first." Will said walking to the sink in the kitchen.

Dee turned on the television so we could all play on the PlayStation. I beat the shit out of Dee and Will playing NBA Live 2003. For the rest of the day we chilled passing jays between us while laughing with one another. When Jimmy came back we gave him a nice fifty piece plus twenty dollars as we planned out what we wanted to do for the rest of the night.

Chapter Six

It was a few more weeks until school began. Me, and the boys had the block on lock. Every bone-crack head in the area was copping from us. We shared shifts and any of the sells on our phones was personal. Man worked from twelve in the afternoon until seven pm. at night. I worked the graveyard shift. But majority of the time we all worked together. When we felt tired, or the Feds were hot on the block we would go to Jimmy's house trapping it out. We was hustling so much we flipped our money four, five times giving us plenty of money to spend. Even though we still had work to flip, we decided to take a break. Our attire always had to stay fresh so we went to the mall to do a bit of early school shopping, and our knowing Will he was not going another week without getting the new Jordan's that had just come out.

<u>Will</u>

All this hustling was paying off because I had so much money. I was ready to spend that shit, and get fresh. We all decided to hit the mall. I opened my shoe box grabbing myself four stacks. My plan was to get Dee and Man both hip to this new style I was starting. When we arrived to the mall I went straight to the G-star shop and they followed suit. We stayed in the mall booking girls, buying shoes and going in and out of every store possible for a few hours. It was a long day and I was ready to get to work replenishing the money I had just spent, smoke some more Purp, and then get back to chilling.

Man

This nigga Will, had us in every store possible both trying on, and buying clothes. Some of that shit was tight fitting as fuck, but I still bought it all because the women were on that nigga Will's style hard. If that can get me more pussy in high school I definitely was going to rock that shit to a *T* like he did. When we made our way over to the Foot Action store I had noticed Dee buying a pair of Pink Jordan 4's. But I knew that nigga was not going to go that hard on wearing some Pink J's. I knew he had something up his sleeve. I was going to find out.

<u>**Dee**</u>

When we walked into Foot Action I seen these hitting ass Jordan's calling out my name. After asking the sales associate to find my size, I came across a pair of Pink Jordan 4's that matched my own and I instantly thought about my baby-girl China, my knowing it would be a nice surprise to make up for the lack of time I had spent with her. When we were back around the way I made it a point giving her a call asking her out. She agreed.

"Meet me at the Malcolm X Park. We need to talk." I told her sounding serious.

"What's wrong Dee?"

"Nothing. Please just meet me there in twenty minutes." *Click.*

I sat in the park waiting on her to arrive. I put the box behind me and proceeded to roll a jay. When I had finished rolling I lit it up. My body relaxed. I finally saw her coming across the park towards me. I stood giving her a long passionate kiss. I almost forgot I was holding the jay in my hand. We sat and talked while I smoked. When I had finished the jay I tossed it away before my picking up the box handing it over to her. She looked inside being shocked at what she saw. I wiped at the tears that welled in her eyes. A few tears eased their way slowly down her cheeks. I wiped them away while my teasing her. "I am not taking you anywhere with me crying like a baby." She stood up from the bench we were then sitting on and began jumping all over me with joy. She kissed me all over telling me that no one had ever done anything like that for her before. We rode over to *Gallery Place* on the train. It was packed like a dozen crabs in a box. Once there we stopped to eat lunch before going to the movies. We were seated in the theatre when she decided to shock the hell out of me. She began playing with my manhood and when she felt it getting hard she dived right in as if she were a professional swimmer looking for gold.

"Oh shit." I whispered grabbing at her hair.

Slurp...slurp...slurp. The sound of her sucking my manhood excited me more increasing my arousal. I grabbed at her hair tightening my fist around some of the strands as she took in each and every drop of my kids into of her mouth. When she came up for air she had swallowed it all smoothly down her throat. When the movie had ended I had to ask her how she had learned to do that technique, because when we first met she told me she never ate before.

"You got *skillz*, Shorty?" I was trying to make it sound more of a compliment. Not a question. I zipped up my pants.

"I read about it from a book titled *Twingasm*. I learned a lot." She licked her lips.

I did not know how many chapters were in that book, but I hoped that she was still reading and learning more. As happy as I was that China and I had spent some quality time together again, it was back to the money I had to go.

Chapter Seven

School was beginning in two days. I decided to spend some time with my mother because I had not seen her in awhile. My mother was a very nice woman who had weaned herself off of drugs. It was because of her addiction that I had been living with my Granny. After I was born in 1988 *the Crack era,* was at an all-time high, so I guess it was easy for my mother to fall right into that habit. I can remember days and nights when I did not see, or hear from her due to her extensive drug habit. After my endless efforts of begging and pleading for her to stop, she finally would, but only to disappear without my knowledge of knowing where or why, which left me extremely broken-hearted. Upon her returning into my life at a much later time she was fully employed, and completely substance free with her skin having a beautiful glow. For a long while I had held onto my resentment hindering our relationship. I chose to continue living with my grandmother even after she had rented her new apartment. It was only after my mother had given birth to my little sister that we began to talk more bringing our relationship closer. As the months went on I became more comfortable in our relationship to feel that I could talk to her about anything, and everything. I did not keep anything from her that had related to my money, the drugs, girls and sex, or about my father. When I finally chose to stay at her place she had given me my own room with a television with a game system set up. I had not expected anything from her, but I appreciated it.

"Junior!" My mother called from the kitchen.

"Yeah ma?

I left my room where I found her in the kitchen washing her hands. She moved a few pots and pans around on the stove before she asked me to be seated at the table.

"What did you decide to do about your school?" She leaned her lower back against the sink while drying her hands on a towel.

"School begins on Monday. I'm going to Wilson High School. Hopefully play B-ball."

"Okay. That sounds nice. I was just making sure." She smiled showing me that she was proud.

"Ma…can I ask you one question?" I flipped the conversation.

"Anything baby."

"Would you want for me to stay here with you?" Although I was slightly afraid to hear her answer, a part of me needed to know.

"Junior of course!" She was a bit surprised that I had asked my question, but she understood all the reasons why I felt the need in asking. "It would be your decision to make."

We ate our dinner together before my returning to my bedroom where I rolled a jay smoking it alone in the bathroom. I thought long and hard as I inhaled, then exhaled the Dro.

On the first day of the beginning of school Man, Will, Moe and myself met up together before our hopping onto the H4bus going to Wilson along with some others from around the way. This was my first year, and I did not have a clue as to what to expect. All I knew was me and my goons were as fly as doves, and we were ready to have fun and clown around.

Will

This was my second year attending Wilson and I was ready to turn my swag up. Last year I flew under the radar as a freshman, but after getting money all summer and now having Man and Dee with me, I knew I was going to be fucking with the most popular bitches this year. When we walked through the doors I felt every eye on us possible. I was Burberry down from head to toe. I was feeling as if I were the freshest nigga in the building. Everything about me screamed money with a big ass M. We walked around looking for three lockers that were close together. With our finding only two that were next to one another we decided to share those on the second floor while keeping one on the first floor by the side exit door just in case of an emergency such as hiding the drugs and shit.

Man

After half the day was gone we ate then walked onto the football field where it was packed with people throwing footballs, walking the track, and girls gossiping and giggling.

"Man watch out!" Dee yelled.

I was not paying attention and before I knew it I pumped right into this beautiful light-skinned girl who was also in my homeroom class by the name of Christine.

"Oh damn. I'm so sorry. Let me help you up." I reached out my hand helping her to her feet.

"It's no problem." She smiled looking at me in my eyes.

My looking at her I felt as though the old saying *love at first sight* was really true.

"I'm Sean, but they call me Man."

"Nice to meet you Man, I'm Christine."

They shook hands as the bell rung.

"Well I need to go to class now. Nice to meet you again." She smiled at him again as she walked off into the building.

Man spun around looking for Dee and Will, but they were nowhere in sight. He ran inside of the building to his locker not wanting to be late for his class on the first day.

"Damn where did ya'll niggas go?" Man said to Dee and Will.

They looked at Man and burst into laughing.

"Let me find out that Mr. Sean got nervous." Dee said still laughing.

Man pushed Dee and smiled.

"Did ya'll see her? She was bad." Man said.

"Yeah nigga we seen the same thing you saw." Will said teasing Man as they exited leaving to attend their classes.

Once the school day ended Will, Man and Dee met up at the front of the school

"My phone has been blowing up like shit." Dee conversed to Man and Will as they rode the H4 back around the way on the crowded bus that was infested with teenagers.

They all agreed as they each had found on their phones missed calls that came from many people that they had dealings with every day selling to them the goods they both needed and wanted. What they did not know and what the movies could not teach them was being in the game of selling drugs was a full time job. The minute you dared to slip up someone with more hunger was always waiting to take your spot to shine.

Chapter Eight

A few months had passed by and everyone was pretty much comfortable being at Wilson to the point where everybody knew everyone. Dee and Man began skipping classes that they had no interest in, affording them both the free time to smoke and chill with other people that chose to do the same thing. Even though Dee did skip his classes he always made sure his grades averaged to a 2.0, so that he could continue to play ball. Will on the other hand, he was a lady's man. He knew the ladies were always in class, and that was where Will's ass would be…in class flirting with all the ladies. Tryouts for basketball were coming up soon. All you heard talk about was how good Wilson was going to be, and who the players were for the team. Dee laughed at the rumors about him not having game anymore. He had stopped playing and the rumor had been that the championship they *"supposedly"* had won was said to have been a fake. What people did not know about Dee was that he was building a drug empire and B-ball had become a part-time job for him. But he never once lost his game. He just wanted finer things for him and his boys. They were all going to find out sooner or later at the tryouts that Dee was hands down the best all-around basketball player attending that school. And whoever would play alongside of him was going to become better because of him.

Dee rose early feeling extremely good for one because he had made lots of money during the previous night. Number two, he was going to dog whoever got in his way of the competition at the tryouts. He grabbed the Nike box that was underneath his bed pulling out his lucky pair of Nike Uptempo's putting them into his bag. He grabbed a Purp jay and a blunt before his calling Man.

"Hello!" Man answered with a crusty voice.

"Wake your ass up nigga." Dee said laughing.

"Nigga- it's still early as shit. I'm going back to sleep." Man said dozing off.

Dee knew what to say to wake Man up. He was going to see if it still worked.

"Well I am about to spark this blunt of Purp up, so if you decide you want to wake up…come on. If not…I'll see you later." Dee said hanging up.

Dee turned on the big screen television turning to the MTV jams channel. While looking at the new *Lil Wayne* video he sparked up the joint. Midway into smoking the blunt, Man walked into Dee's bedroom. He locked the door before his flopping down upon the lazy boy chair Dee had in his room.

"Pass that shit over here." Man said reaching his hand. "What the hell are you doing up so early anyway? School not going to start for another damn two and a half hours." He grabbed the blunt taking two strong pulls off of it.

Dee exhaled the smoke from his mouth before speaking.

"I need to be ready because it's try-outs today. I will be eating early today." Dee grabbed the blunt from Man's hand. And by the way, I made a killing last night fucking around with Jimmy and them."

When the blunt was finished Dee and Man both sat looking at the television stuck somewhere between earth and space. The ringtone sounded on Dee's cellphone. (*I move chickens-I move chickens-I move chickens*).

"Yo Man...you are sitting on my phone...so you need to answer it." Dee said still looking at the television high as a kite.

"Who is this?" Man asked not recognizing the number that appeared on the phone.

Fiz laughed. "This Fiz."

"Oh shit! What's up Fiz? Yo' this is Man. Hold on a sec… here go Dee." He passed the phone.

"Sup Big cuz." Dee asked.

"Shit. "He said partially laughing. "I know you got some trees. Where you at?" Fiz asked.

"I'm over gramps house. Come through."

"Okay I'll be there in ten minutes. Tell Man to get his lazy ass up, and come out too. I need to holla at ya'll anyway."

Dee turned looking towards Man to deliver the message. "Fiz said get ready to come outside." He then returned speaking to Fiz. "Okay Cuz, we going to be ready."

"Oh yeah…and by the way I will be in a white Benz." *Click*.

Man left out heading back to his place to get himself together before he started his morning off with the boys, then school. Dee rushed to wash his face and to brush his teeth before his phone went off again letting him know that Fiz was waiting. Dee grabbed 7grams of Purp, and a 3.5 gram of some KB (*Kind Bud*) before he left to go outside to meet Fiz. When Dee and Man stepped outside of the building all their ears could hear was the loud booming of speakers echoing in the air. *I shoot your…arm…leg, leg…arm…head. The heater burner bruisa is on my hip this year. Dressed in all black, and my gun the same color.*

When Fiz spotted them coming towards the car he turned the music down before his getting out of the Benz. He greeted both Dee and Man with a hug giving them some dap.

"Ya'll get inside." Fiz told them as he moved back into the drivers' seat

Dee and Man followed moving to get into the car. Man in the backseat with Dee up front with Fiz. They sat talking for a few minutes before Fiz pulled off with all of them together in the car.

"I have been hearing good things about ya'll since I have been gone." Fiz commented.

"Like what?" Dee asked trying to fiqure out what his cousin knew or had heard about them.

"I had people telling me that ya'll are making big boy moves in the drug game. That ya'll are the ones who have the neighborhood on lock. Before you say anything I want ya'll to know it's in your blood to be bosses, but be careful because there are a lot of snakes slithering in the grass." Fiz told them.

Man looked at Dee and gave him the nod to let Fiz know what's really good.

"Well Cuz, we really don't have the block on lock, but we do take turns selling that Kim K."

"Fuck that. Let's get something to eat and we'll talk all about it after a full stomach." Man said cutting them off from talking. "And turn that weezy back up." Man said laughing happily to see his old head back in good shape.

Fiz looked at Dee then at Man. "I missed ya'll young-ins." He said before turning the Carter 1 on.

"Hey Fiz…take us over to the Steak and Eggs for breakfast since we have to be at school. It will be on the way. We can eat, smoke and talk." Man told him.

After eating a good morning meal, Man pulled a stack of Dubs (*twenty dollar bills*) out of his pocket paying for everything. When Fiz saw how Man carried it by paying for their meals he earned a lot more respect for them. It had also solidified the rumors he had heard about them to being true. Once they had finished with eating their meals they walked back to the car so Fiz could drive them to school. Parking two blocks away

Fiz turned the car off and Dee pulled the weed out from his backpack.

"Damn Cuz! What you want for a 3.5 of that Purp shit? Fiz asked while he closely examined the purple greenish looking weed.

Man burst out laughing at Fiz.

"Cuz…It's free for you! You don't have to hit none with us, cause we gonna' spark that KB with you." Dee said breaking the KB up in a fifty dollar bill.

"Man rolled a couple of sheets and funnel jays for me." Dee said as he passed Man the KB.

"I am on it now." Man told him as he rolled jay after jay.

We sat in the car relaxing as smoked filled the atmosphere. Easing my seat back and leaning I turned the radio up a few octaves as Dipset beat hit the speakers, and Jim Jones spit that fly guy shit.

"I know ya'll had something to do with those killings that went down the night I got shot."

"What? You trippin' Fiz. What makes you think we had something to do with that?" Man asked reaching for the jay.

"Cause I know the love ya'll got for me. And because that very same night I had blown my aunt's phone up looking for Dee. I know he did not come home until later that night after the shooting took place on 13th and G Street."

"Okay Cuz, it don't matter now as long as you good." Dee sparked up the other jay.

Man asked him while his looking high as a kite. "What… time is… it?" He looked around for his phone.

"It's 9:20am." Fiz told him.

"Okay. I'm high…as shit." Dee said as he sparked the last jay they had rolled. "Cuz, after we smoke this jay can you take us over to the CVS before dropping us in front of the school?" Dee passed the jay to his cousin Fiz waiting for an answer.

"Of course Dee. I was going to ask what ya'll wanted me to do anyway." Fiz told him hitting the jay a couple of times before his passing it to Man.

After the jay was gone Fiz started the car up. He drove down 33rd street to the CVS. When Man spotted Christine, a classmate from his school crossing the street he eased the window down..

"Good morning. Can I walk with you?"

When she realized it was Man who was talking to her she said good morning back with a huge smile.

"Of course Sean. Come on."

Dee and Fiz looked at one another. The look of shock on their faces was crazy because Man's birth name Sean was only heard out loud when his mother was calling for him.

Fiz dropped Dee off in front of the school.

"See you later Fiz." Man said.

"Cuz…I am going to hit you up later, but if you need me I'm a phone call away." Fiz told him before pulling off.

Before going inside the building Dee received a text from Will.

Aye Dee. I'm not coming to school. I don't feel well today.

He texted him back: *Okay Will I'll hold it down for you. Feel better son.*

He returned a text: *Thanks a lot homie. Good luck and bust those boys' asses on the court.*

Chapter Nine

It seemed as if tryouts was a five on five game. A lot of people had stayed after school to see the competition. Since the coach already knew who Dee was he made him a captain along with the star player, Shadog from the previous year. The funny thing about it was, Shadog and Dee knew one another. Shadog was older than Dee, but he was also from around the way.

"Freshman get to pick first." Shadog said as he passed the ball to Dee.

Dee's eyes scanned around the gym looking at the many people that had come to the tryouts before making his decision.

"I'll take the white boy." Dee said pointing to the young man they knew as Paul Young.

After their choosing their teams the game went to 11 by ones and twos only.

"Ya'll can have the ball first." Dee said.

The game became real rough minded for Dee. One- because this was his first game in a while and two- he needed to get a feel for the game before it got too late. Dee missed his first two shots and he went down 3-0. The next play he came down, faked a shot and found Paul in the corner for a two pointer. Shadog tried to blow passed Dee, but Dee had stuck his right hand out, and the ball went loose. Dee's team mate Speedie retrieved the ball and seen to Dee for a fast break lay-up. They all went back and forth playing good defense. Coach J. watched while his charting things down as he saw his future team playing against one another with their all. Dee's team went down ten to eight. Dee had the ball. After passing it over to Paul, he then ran around a screen block Speedie had made. Paul passed it back to Dee at the side of the court. Dee fired up an opened two pointer that went straight through the net. After coach J seen that he blew his whistle.

"Let me get five laps." He yelled out before his going into his office.

"Good shot." Shadog said to Dee as they ran the laps side by side. "I thought you had lost it after that brawl at the game. I have not seen you play a game all summer."

"Thanks Dog. I know. I fell off, but I'll pick it back up sooner, or later."

"We was some shit last year, but with Paul…we might easily take the championship together."

Shadog said after they had done the laps. "How are you getting home?"

"I'm not sure, but maybe by bus, or by the train. Why whadd-up?" Dee questioned.

"I'll get Paul to take us home since you live right down the street from me. I'll tell him to drop you off down at the Rec, or wherever you want to go."

Paul pulled up in his ride.

"Yo Paul can Dee catch a ride with us?'

"Yeah Dog. It's no problem. Good game Bro." Dog said to Dee giving him some dap.

For the next few weeks tryouts got tougher and the teams changed. On the last day of tryouts the coach sat everybody down in the stands and made a loud speech that meant a lot.

Coach J.

After watching the talented skills from these young men over the last few days, my assistant and I had to make a decision in the selecting of twelve players for the JV team and twelve also for the Varsity team. This was always the most difficult part of my job to do because I liked them all regardless of whether they had the ball skills or not. Their mothers' or fathers' always wanted to know why their kid had not made my roster. I hated to see the disappointed looks on their faces when I had to tell them that being good was simply just not good enough. After my assistant and I were both in agreement that we had selected the best twenty-four students for our school team I had to make my speech.

"Everybody please take a seat and calm down. I am very appreciative that you all came every day to the tryouts playing your hearts out. But at the end of the day, as you all know, there will be only twenty-four of you men that are going to be able to make my roster. You did your best, so don't become angry with me, or with yourselves if you don't make it. You always have next year to try-out. Tomorrow the names for JV and Varsity teams will be posted on the side of the gym doors during lunchtime. Good luck men and thank you again for trying out for the Woodrow Wilson Tigers."

It seemed as if the morning was moving extra slow until lunchtime as Dee waited for the bell to ring. He felt optimistic about his chances for making the team even though he had two bad days prior. At least that was what he thought.

Ring ring ring

The bell rang and everyone jetted out the door for lunch. Dee went to his locker to meet Man and Will who were talking to two girls.

"What's up Dee?"

They both gave him dap.

"I am tired as hell from Ms. Swan's class." Dee told them as he opened the locker throwing his math book into the bottom of it.

"Hey. Your name Dee Morrison?" One of the girls inquired.

"Yeah. Why you asking sweetheart?" He asked while turning to face her.

"I think I had seen your name on one of those B-Ball sheets posted on the gym door earlier." She said smiling.

"Oh yeah. Thank you." Dee said before closing his locker shut. "What ya'll eating for lunch?"

Both Will and Man shrugged their shoulders indicating that they didn't know.

"Well, I am ordering some pizza hut." Dee said pulling his phone from his pocket.

He walked away taking steps down the hallway towards the exit doors. When he was outside he ran into Paul.

"*Sup'* Paul?"

"I'm just chilling. I was about to leave to get myself something to eat."

"Damn. That makes two of us. I am about to do the same thing."

"Do you smoke? Paul asked completely out of the blue while they were walking to his car.

"Of course. You know somebody who don't?" Dee laughed at the ridiculous question.

Paul had no idea that Dee was the future Plug for the Loud Pack.

"If you want too... we can match, or something."

"Okay cool. Where you trying to eat at?" Dee felt the growling in his stomach.

"It don't matter to me bro. Did you know we made the team? And for some reason there was a star beside our names too? Paul started up his car.

"I heard we made the team, but what's the star about." Dee was confused.

"Don't know. I got me some White Owls if that is cool with you? While we are smoking we can put our order in for our meals before we get there." Paul turned off onto a side street where he parked the car. "Come on."

Paul and Dee began walking towards a large home that Dee imagined he would only see in a movie. Once Paul opened the front door they were greeted by a charging Pit Bull that made Dee's heart jump quickly skipping miles, but to his surprise the dog was friendly.

"Nice house."

"Lock the bottom lock" Paul said to him as he went into the kitchen bringing back two power-aids. "Come on."

Dee followed Paul down to the basement. They both went inside a room that had chairs along with a radio.

They began rolling up a jay of some nice Loud Pack that Paul took from a bottom drawer.

"This your crib?" Dee asked seeing his future.

"Family house." Paul told him as he rolled the jay.

"Cool." Dee pulled out the rest of the buds he had from the other day. You can roll this up too since you already rolling up."

Dee passed the orange-greenish bud on to Paul. Paul looked it over as if he was examining it.

"Good looking weed."

After they smoked chilling for a minute, it was time to hit the Pizza Hut before their heading back to the school.

At the end of the school day, Dee, Shadog and Paul had to meet with Coach J in his office. Neither of them had any awareness of what the meeting was about.

Knock... knock... knock...

"Come in. You guys have a seat."

They each pulled a chair from the stack piled in the corner of his office.

"I called you three men to my office because I'm sure you have all seen the stars beside your names and are wondering why they are there. I believe this school has a great chance to bring a DCIAA Championship to this organization. I would like to extend an offer to the three of you to be my captains."

Dee, Paul, along with Shadog, sat there quiet. They were stunned with hearing what the coach was offering to them.

"Well coach I gladly appreciate your offer, but I need time to think about this before making a decision. And if you don't mind I would also like to talk it over with these guys." Dee said looking at each of them.

"I don't have a problem with that at all. You guys just keep in mind that an offer such as this only comes once in a lifetime."

They all stood including the coach. Coach J thanked them all for coming giving each of them a firm handshake as they left out from his office.

"Dee what was that all about?" Shadog asked as they walked out of the building heading over to the train station.

"I will talk to you about that later. Just know I did make the right decision for us." Dee said to them.

"Aye Dee and Shadog, ya'll need a ride home, or something?" Paul offered as he stood waiting at his car door.

"Nah, we good for now." Shadog responded back at him giving him some dap.

"I'll catch you on Monday." Dee gave Paul dap also.

"Aye…Dee you got a phone?" Paul pulled his phone from his back pocket.

"Yeah. Take my number down."

Dee gave him his number knowing that it was all about the Loud Pack.

"Okay I will hit ya'll up later."

Paul slid behind the wheel and into the drivers' seat before his driving away.

Chapter Ten

Dee was busy all week with basketball tryouts, but he still somehow managed to sell his drugs late night. They were making so much money they could not believe how many shoeboxes they had filled with the, Benjamins. Dee had the weekend all to himself with nothing much to do. He called his boys so they could hang out and begin planning the next steps they were going to take in selling drugs.

Dee had just arrived over to his grandmother's building when he saw Man's big sister Patrice. For years Dee had tried to get at her despite the fact that his right hand man did not approve of it. It was something about this girl that screamed to Dee. He anxiously wanted to test the waters with her.

"What's up Patrice? Where is Man at?"

"He left out of the house already with some girl from his school...or from somewhere." Patrice looked him up and down.

"Oh yeah. When you *gonna* let me kick it with you?" he said with all smiles while looking at her sexually.

"Sorry Dee. Just because of the fact you are in high school now does not mean you can hang."

She said blowing him a kiss goodbye before her walking away.

"Yeah okay. We'll see about that." He yelled back at her before she was out of earshot.

Quickly pausing in her steps she turned around to face him. "We will see then." She continued walking away again.

Will

Things has been so hectic lately I have not even been able to chill with my boys except when we are having lunch, or in between our classes at school. I was going to make sure I hit them up over the weekend just to talk about what's been going on and about the many complaints I had been receiving about this last batch of crack we bought.

Man

My last couple of weeks have been heaven. I had been spending a lot of time with Christine and I have to say I'm really feeling her. She is different. She is bi-racial mixed with Brazilian and White blood. Her eyes are green and she is definitely the '*baddest bitch*' in the building. Lately I have been spending so much time with her that my boys have been placed on the back burner, my drugs have been sitting, and I have been blowing more money like crazy. But who cares when you got a bad bitch?

<u>Dee</u>

Although, I have not heard anything from Man yet, Will and I together decided we would meet over Jimmy's house just to kick it for a minute talking about the future we got going on.

When Dee and Will arrived at Jimmy's as they had planned, something was very strange when they knocked on Jimmy's door.

Knock… knock… knock…

"I think I can hear somebody breathing." Will had placed his ear against the door.

"If Jimmy wants to play games then fuck him." Dee said as they both started to walk away before they heard the door opening.

"Aye." Jimmy stood at the door wincing in pain.

Dee and Will both turned around walking back towards Jimmy.

"What's wrong with you Jimmy?" Will asked.

"Long story. But I will tell ya'll about it in a minute. Fasten the top bolt and chain lock the door for me, Dee."

They all settled down on the couch and Jimmy went right into telling them all about what had happened.

"I been owing this kid they call Pun for months now a fucking fifty bucks. I had been making so much money in the past six months working with Dee and them, that the fifty dollars had not even crossed my mind. I didn't even need to go over to 17th and Euclid anymore because I had an overflow of people hitting my phone up and coming over to me where I stay I forgot about the money honestly because I had not seen him. You know the saying *out of sight out of mind.* Last week been hell for me. Dee been busy with school, Man been with some new girl and Will gave me some garbage, so I had to buy some Torch, for myself, or I was going to lose my freakin' mind. I called John because I knew he stayed with the best and he told me to meet him on Fuller. When I arrived it was a gang of them shooting dice. John met me and I bought me a twenty piece and walked off. Before I got to the corner Pun called out my name and told me to come here. At first he was cool.

"Jimmy-Where my money at?"

So I asked him because I was confused. "What money?"

"Jimmy…I see you think I'm playing with you, but you owe me from a couple of months ago. I gave you seven Rocks for fifty dollars." Pun told him becoming angry.

"Oh shit! That's my bad Pun. I been so busy. I forgot." Jimmy's face showed stupidity. "Give me a week and I promise I got you Pun."

Pun smirked not giving any consideration to the fact that Jimmy may have been telling the truth. "Okay Jimmy. I can now see how this going. You already got it from me, so now you don't owe me anything anymore." Pun had fire in his eyes.

When Jimmy turned around Pun pulled his 32 off his waist and shot Jimmy right in his ass.

"Nigga, that's a booty wound for fucking with the money you owed to me." Pun lashed out at him as he walked away with a smoking gun in his hand.

Jimmy walked about a block before he really felt the pain of the injury kicking in. The blood leaked down his leg and Jimmy felt his right leg give way on him. He received help from a pedestrian who was nearby. When he arrived to the hospital he learned from the triage nurse that it had not been a deeply inflicted wound. He was released the next day with a pair of crutches along with a subscription for pain killers.

"So that explains why you just hiding out in the crib. Look at your scary punk ass." Dee was laughing so hard he could not breathe.

"Dee…Fuck you!" Jimmy cursed trying not to laugh while giving Dee the middle finger.

Jimmy hobbled on his crutches into the kitchen to get a drink.

"Aye Dee. Go check out the Live Game Box. It should be a 3.5 of some *Dro* in it." Will said.

Dee checked the box to find a bag of some Dro that had been left from the last time they had smoked together. Dee rolled up two Backwoods as they sat watching television and talked for a minute.

"So what's up with the Coke Fatz sold you?" Dee asked as he sparked the Backwoods up.

"Dee let me tell you. That shit was some pure garbage. Ever since Fatz, and his crew took over the Southside they been giving me the left over shit." Will answered him with frustration.

"Will… you call Fatz. You tell him we need to meet up. We have to talk about the Coke we have been getting from them." Dee took a hit off the jay of Dro.

"Okay. I'll get on it as soon as possible." Will said laughing as he grabbed the jay away from Dee.

"What's up with Man?" Dee asked.

"That nigga gone off of that girl Christine. It's like his nose is wide open for her." Will said coughing off the Hydro.

"Man- that nigga ain't been hitting my phone, or coming around *slim*." Dee added.

"Well don't trip cause I know he been blowing his money like shit, so I know he going to hit one of our phones very soon." Will laughed.

"Oh yeah. By the way… before I forget to tell ya'll… mom's is moving us to a new place on S Street over near Yellow Brick." Will mentioned while taking two more pulls before his putting the jay out.

"Damn. That's crazy. I hope nothing changes and you keep coming around." Dee told him.

With all of them feeling as if they were walking on the moon they begin laughing.

"Well let's get out of here I got some shit I got to handle. Will told them standing up to leave out.

When they parted ways Dee received a call on his phone from a number he did not recognize. He answered to a voice that was unfamiliar.

"Hello?"

"Yo-Dee. What you doing tonight?"

"I don't know. But who is this?"

"My bad son. This is Paul from school."

"Oh shit. What's up? I'm free tonight. Why?"

"Some cheerleader from our school is having a party tonight. I wanted to know if you wanted to go."

"Of course. What time does it start? Better yet where is it?" Dee was all in.

"I think it pops off around eleven. It's over by our school somewhere, but I'll come and get you in an hour. Do you have some Loud Pack, or do you know where to get it from?"

Dee laughed at the ridiculous question. "Don't worry about the Loud. It's on me tonight."

"Okay cool. I'll meet you down by the Rec and I'll call you when I am there." Paul said before his hanging up the phone.

Dee quickly took a shower before putting on his Lacrosse gear. Before his leaving out he reached inside his shoebox grabbing an ounce of some Purp Buds before his stopping to spray on a dash of his Hugo Boss cologne. When Dee arrived to the party it was a scene from a fucking movie. There were people playing beer pong, girls were dancing everywhere, bowls of weed, and I did say girls were everywhere.

"Do you want something to drink?" Paul asked Dee.

"Yeah. Get me what you are drinking."

"Are you sure?"

"Yeah. And we got next on the table." Dee told him while looking at the game being played at the beer pong table.

While Dee waited for Paul to bring the drinks it seemed as if everybody knew who he was. Girls he had never spoken with in school now seemed as though they knew him and wanted to say hey. Dee moved on through the room before seating himself on a couch nearby where other people were smoking. He pulled out the Purp and in no time he had rolled up two Backwoods jays before Paul had returned.

"Yo- Dee! Let's make a toast to the good life." Paul said as he handed the Dee the cup so they could both toast.

Dee drank from his cup immediately tasting the burn of the alcohol. "Damn- What in the f...uck is this shit?" He lit the jay.

"It is some Grey Goose. Why? Is it too strong?" Paul laughed.

"Nah." Dee took a hit from the Backwoods that he just sparked.

Just as he passed Paul the jay the crowd went wild in the room. Whoop Whoop!!! The game was over. Paul and Dee had the next game. The game started out fast and before he knew it, Dee was drinking two cups of beer at the same time. It was a blessing that Paul knew what he was doing because Dee was feeling lit, and he knew if Dee had drank a couple more beers he would have been finished for the entire night. When the game ended people moved themselves into smaller groups chilling, smoking, drinking and popping pills. When the night ended Dee had made a lot of friends for his business. He knew it was time he take his drug game to the next level. When

Paul had dropped him off it was after five in the morning and the sun would soon rise. Still both high and drunk, Dee stayed on the fire escape firing up his last Backwoods jay. Before he was halfway into the Purp, Man came from out of nowhere and sat next to him.

"Pass that shit." Man grabbed the weed out of his hand.

"Damn nigga. You could have said what's up first." And where the fuck have you been?"

"Around." Man hit the Purp passing it back to Dee.

Dee was feeling so good from his high he did not even respond to him when the jay was done. He went into his apartment fell across the top of his bed crashing. When he had awakened hours later he noticed he had ten missed calls along with three voice messages.

"Damn...I must have been tired as shit. He said while yawning and stretching his arms above his head.

It was eight o'clock and Dee wasted no time in returning the missed calls he had received from Will. Will answered his cellphone on the third ring.

"What's up Dee? Where you at?"

"I'm in the crib son. I was sleeping."

"Well...I am on my way over there. Have you seen Man yet?"

"Yeah. He should be in the house. Why?"

"Just hit him up on his cell. Tell him to be over your house..." Will looked down at his watch. "...in twenty."

Before his jumping into the shower Dee took a minute sending Man a text telling him to meet at his house in twenty. Dee had lost track of the time while he was singing in the shower. The twenty minutes passed quickly by because when he came out of the bathroom Man was already there in his room sitting in the Lazy Boy chair watching MTV Jams.

"Where is Will? Dee scanned the room for any signs that he was around.

"I think he went into your kitchen to get some water." Man leaned forward as if he was being disturb while watching the show.

Minutes later as Dee sat putting on his shoes Will came into the room.

"What's up Slim?" Will gave Dee both dap and a brotherly hug. "What's good for tonight?"

"We are going over to the Southside to meet up with Phil and Fatz." Will slipped his shirt over his head.

Dee grabbed a couple of stacks of Benjamins and grabbed his fitted hat that accommodated his outfit.

"So I am lost?" Man said scratching at his head. "Why in the hell are we going to Southside? Is there something I missed out on?" Man asked looking at both Dee and Will for answers.

"Look Man, you the one who has been missing out because of some pussy you probably did not even hit yet, so just look and pay attention." Dee said to him laughing.

"So how are we going to get there?" Dee asked.

Oh yeah…my bad. I forgot to tell ya'll I just bought a car." Will smiled.

Dee and Man looked at one another before they both burst into a cry of laughter.

"You don't even know how to drive fool." Dee reminded him.

"I know this man. That's why you are going to drive. And you are going to teach me too."

"Do I look like I am your Chauffeur?"

Will stroked his imaginary beard before telling him…you do look a bit like Morgan Freeman."

"Who you think you driving Miss Daisy?"

They all laughed again.

They gathered their necessities leaving to head over to Southside. Just as they were about to exit the building Dee turned running back down to the basement grabbing his stash along with two straps. Making their way out to the car Dee gave Man one of the straps before his placing the nine millimeter in his lap as they pulled off.

Dee pressed his finger on the button turning on the radio. "Damn Will, what made you buy this car?"

"I saw it on Craigslist for the low."

Will had wasted no time hooking his phone up to the USB cord that was in the car. Will turned the volume up high as the radio played Lil Wayne's *Money on My Mind*. When they pulled up and had found a parking space Will called Fatz to tell him he was on his way up. Fatz told him to be careful. He also instructed him to get off the elevator on the eighth floor, then to walk up one flight of steps to 912. Dee put the strap on his hip before getting out the car. As they walked closer to the building a group of dudes were hanging out in front. As they moved cautiously beyond them they felt the tension in the air. Dee gave Man the eye letting him know he needed to keep his guard up. When they were standing at the elevator doors waiting for them to open, two of the dudes walked up behind them waiting as well. When the doors opened Dee walked in first. He moved to the back. The other two guys stepped in. When the doors closed Dee planted his hand on the Dog he had to be sure nothing fishy was about to go down before his pressing the arrow to go up. When the elevator came to a stop the doors re-opened, but the two dudes who had followed them must have re-evaluated the position they had placed themselves in because they remained on the elevator waiting for the doors to close again. Dee's body language had sent them a clear message that he was not in the mood for the bull-shit, but he would gladly take a nigga out if at all necessary. They continued moving along just as Fatz had instructed them to do without anymore interruptions. When they had finally reached the door numbered 912, Will knocked three times giving Phil the signal letting him know that it was them. The door opened slowly allowing them to walk in. Inside it was as if they had just entered into a steamy strip club. Phil, G, Fatz, and Jeezy were seated watching a game while half-naked women within the room sat around drinking and talking shit among one another. When the game went into half-time they all stepped into another room where there was a stripper pole next to the bed.

"Come in and close the door behind you." Fatz said speaking to G.

We all sat down on the carpet.

"So what is good with ya'll?" Fatz asked.

"We need some better Coke Fatz. That last shit was trash. It ran some crackheads away." Will's face showed seriousness.

"Damn that's my bad." Fatz admitted to them. "Well look here since that was on me I'll give ya'll three ounces on the strength." he added.

"Dee- what type of straps ya'll got on you?" Phil waited for Dee to respond with an answer.

Dee pulled the 9mm off his waist handing it to Phil.

"Damn! I heard ya'll got shit on lock since we left." He returned the Glock to Dee.

"Nah. We just trying to make ends meet." Will stated so nonchalantly making everyone laugh repeatedly while giving each other dap.

"Aye Jeezy, let me buy some of that gas you got."

"Man, I don't have no more Purp. But what I do have is some OG Kush." Jeezy walked to the closet then threw Man a half of a pound.

"*Whooo…* This will definitely do." Man pulled some Franklins out giving them to Jeezy.

"Well we gotta get out of here." Will grabbed the dope from Fatz.

Before they left Fatz's place, G told them he had some Choppers for sale that were legitimate, so they needed to be sure to get at him.

"We will get at you the next time we come up here. Everybody be safe." Will said as his eyes crossed paths with all the homies in the room.

When they left out from the building that very same tension that was in the air when they had arrived was still there only this time the nigga's looked as if they were plotting hard. Dee, Will and Man walked passed them. It had become obvious from all the whispering that something was about to go down. Before they had walked ten feet along the sidewalk, a kid with dark skin approached them asking them where they were from. Dee gave Will the nod for him to just keep walking when someone yelled out "That's those nigga's that be uptown." The shadows moving along the brick wall of the building were a dead giveaway to give Dee and Man a heads up that they needed to think about about making a move soon. Dee and Man spun around and yelled, "We from *1-7* nigga." as they pulled their glocks out continuously firing while running with speed to the car. Dee jumped in behind the wheel with Man jumping in beside him on the passenger side. Will leaped into the back seat just as Dee hit the floor pedal and sped off. When Dee had driven two blocks away he placed the heated Dog beneath the drivers' seat. His heart was beating at a fast pace in his chest. Dee tightly gripped the steering wheel as the car turned every corner with the four tires screeching as they burned rubber. He maneuvered the vehicle as if he were competing in the Indie 500 race. Once they were beyond any danger he tried masking his own nervousness by keeping his vision pinned straight ahead. He looked out through the windshield and onto the road ahead, wondering whether both Will and Man were feeling the same way.

"Whoo… oh man. When we walked passed them nigga's I thought they were going to try to rob us." Will expressed with his heart still racing.

Man spoke up. "Their asses were not going to rob shit! They had another thought coming if they thought that." Man showed no fear in his voice.

"Will, did you make sure you still have that dope in your jacket? You were running a little fast. We can't afford another loss."

"I still got it with me Dee. I was holding on to it as if it was my life. It's all good."

"Nigga it was your life." Man said while causing laughter releasing tears and all the tension that had been bottled up in the car. They each relived their own recollections of the night while teasing one another about who had been the most afraid.

Chapter Eleven

School was going good for Dee, Will and Man, but their outside hustle was going even better. The Coke that Fatz was bringing to the table was fire, and every crackhead on the East Coast was traveling to get a hold of that Pack from Dee and the crew. It had come to a point where Dee and Man began to miss days of school because their phones was jumping. Dee even hooked up with his own *Plug* that sold E pills at its purest form for just a dollar a pill as long as he bought one thousands of them thanks to Paul. When Dee drove over the bridge to Virginia to meet up with his *Plug* named Zac he took twenty-five thousand dollars with him just in case. But to Dee's surprise Zac sold him two-thousand pills throwing in an additional two-thousand telling him to just get back at him. When Dee returned to the city he parked down at the Rec in back of the Condo building. He pulled out two large Zip-locked bags filled with different pills. He sat looking at the multiple colors and labels on the pills that were in front of him. It amazed him seeing pills which had symbols such as stars, Superman emblems, #1, naked ladies, G's up, Dolphins and more. People wanted to meet up with him everywhere and anywhere to get their hands on one of those blue, red, or white pills from him. When he went to school all the Punk rockers knew who he was and wanted what he had. Dee allowed his curiosity to get the best of him and before he knew it he was popping a blue star pill into his mouth. He needed to understand why everybody was chasing him down for it. For the first fifteen minutes Dee was pissed off he had popped the pill not receiving any instant gratification, but when it finally kicked in he felt as if he were the man of the hour. His swag went from zero to one hundred. Dee decided to walk down to the Rec to meet up with his homies so they could get a bottle and chill on the block as they did on most weekends. When Dee hit the corner he noticed Moe, Will, Man, G and the two new brothers who had just moved around there, Leon and Larry. Dee gave them dap before his getting straight to matters about what he wanted to do.

"Let's walk to the store to get a bottle." Dee said loudly feeling the Ecstasy he had just popped.

They dug into their pockets pulling out money.

 "I got a dub." Man held up his twenty dollar bill showing it.

"Me, and Leon have ten dollars apiece." Larry said as he moved getting up from the steps.

"You need to say no more." Dee said as they started walking in the direction leading them to the neighborhood *Wayne's Liquor* store.

"Give us a bottle of that Remy right there." Dee pointed over the shoulder of the cashier while pulling the money out from his pocket.

"That will be Forty-two dollars." Mr. Wayne, who was the owner told him while pulling the bottle of Remy down from the shelf and placing it along with a pack of cups into a bag.

"Thanks Wayne. I will see you another time."

"Hold up. Before we leave let me get a bottle of that Absolute and two Cranberry juices." Will pulled out his money.

Everyone looked back and forth at one another then back again at Will not believing that he was serious. Will paid for his bottle and they left not saying a word about his unusual purchase. Before they turned onto Kalorama Road to get back onto the block, Dee had spotted a beautiful young lady with long hair. She wore a nose ring, and she had a certain sophistication about her as she walked along with a few other girls. The pill he had taken had now moved through his system and had him in overdrive. Dee walked ahead to stop her.

"Excuse me Beautiful, how are you doing? He grabbed her hand.

"I'm fine… but do I know you?" She looked at Dee inquisitively.

"No. But I am trying to get to know you a lil' bit better." he smiled.

"No thank you." She walked away continuing on with her friends.

Dee made a quick move to walk alongside her.

"Excuse me for coming at you so suddenly like that my African Queen, but my name is Dee."

That stopped her making her smile at him.

"My name is Meme. Nice to meet you Dee."

They exchanged words for a few more minutes before Dee was able to get her number. When Dee arrived back on the block the others had already made it ahead of him and were already pouring their first cup of the alcohol. Dee made it just in time to toast to the good life.

"Will, why did you buy that bottle because you don't drink?"

"Because I am drinking tonight." He turned his cup up chasing the Absolute with the juice.

Dee did not ask him another thing about it. He shrugged his shoulders leaving it at that.

"That bitch you spoke to was bad Dee. Did you get her number?" Larry asked.

"Of course." Dee said feeling himself. "I'm hot as moe kill." He pulled off his shirt.

Dee poured another cup for himself then pulled some sheets and funnel out with a bud of Kush that Man had given him. He rolled it before his walking out front where he sparked the jay. The streets were beginning to crowd with cars and people were moving around up and down the block. When everybody else came outside to the front the bottle was already down half-way and they were all feeling the results. Dee passed the jay over to his boy Man.

"Damn! Now I can see why ya'll be sipping. I'm twisted like a motherfucker." Will said as he walked down the steps.

Man laughed out loud following Will down the steps.

I'm rolling like shit. Dee said only to himself. He pulled his shirt back on as he walked down the steps. "Let's go up top."

Before they walked up the block, G gave them dap and walked down the street in another direction, while Leon and his brother Larry both decided to stay back and eventually went home.

"I'm with it." Moe said running back inside of the building retrieving the bottles they had left behind.

When Moe returned joining them they walked up the street heading towards Seventeenth & Euclid Street where it resembled a ghost town when they had arrived. Dee wondered where everybody could be hanging out, so he called Fiz. Fiz never answered.

"Fuck this shit. Let's go on Fuller and Mozart." Moe said walking through the playground. "I bet they are out there."

It was true. Just as he had said everybody from the block was there. Fiz was talking to some Lil' Shawty, Fatz, Phil, the 1-7 girls was out there. G, and even Lil D. was out there. And you were lucky if you caught up with him because he was always in the studio so much. When Dee walked up it was as if he had saved the night. Everybody wanted a pill to *boot up*. Dee went to Fizs' car, opened the door and when he sat down he took the pills from his socks and gave the block what they were looking for. Girls from Howard had even walked past the block giving the niggas play while still buying what they needed before they went back to the dorm for the night. An hour had past and everyone was in small groups, geeking and tweeking off them *Jegga Joints.* Before Dee, Man and Will's stepping off and moving on, Pun came from around the corner giving everybody dap showing love. When Dee, Pun, Will and Man came face to face they faked mugged before their giving each other some dap.

"I heard ya'll boys got down low on lock now." Pun commented.

Will, Dee and Man looked at each other bursting into laughter.

"Nah. We just cooling Bob." Man said feeling both the drinks and the Pack.

"Well we need to team up and have all this shit on lock. We can always make a *lil' hustle* into something major." Pun said.

The thing Pun did not know was the numbers they were bringing in was major paper. They just kept niggas out of their way and they knew how to invest. Dee took what Pun said keeping it on his mind for the next meeting to come.

"Okay Big Pun we going to talk about it soon. Just stay out the way and we are going to get at you." Dee gave him dap before he stepped off.

Dee's mother was out of town so they hopped in Will's car and crashed up 640 for the night. Before Dee fell asleep he sent a text to the young lady he had seen earlier that night.

I hope you had a nice night beautiful, and made it home safely. Goodnight sweetheart!! From: Dee.

Chapter Twelve

Wilson had a bad start when the b-ball season started. They went two-four losing games to HD Woodson, Dunbar, Blue and Cardoza. Dee was losing focus due to the money he was making and the many late nights he spent on the block. Things took a quick turn when some of the other players started to talk shit to Dee about his lack of skills on the court. So Dee did what he knew best to do. And that was to show them better than he could tell them by carrying the team to a 6 game winning streak. But then the worst thing ever that could happened took place. They were playing Gonzaga High School. Dee had the ball with two minutes left on the clock. He was on fire, scoring 28 points, 6 assists and 10 rebounds. The coach yelled to him to call an isolation play. He crossed to the left backing his opponent down. With his running at full speed he put the ball behind his back moving to the basket and dunking it. He came down stepping to his right on the center of his foot causing him to break his ankle. Shadog, Paul, and the coach rushed to Dee's side. After assessing his injury it was determined that he could not continue to play in the game, so they carried him away from the court. After Dee's arriving by ambulance to the hospital his mother met him there. After a few hours of sitting in the emergency room he was finally released with a pair of crutches and a hard cast. That night he smoked while lying on his mother's couch. He took two pain killers and went to sleep. Dee stayed home that entire week without answering his phone, or going to school. Man and Will became so worried about Dee they went to check on him at his mother's crib over on Morton Street. They banged on the door until Dee finally came to answer their knock. He was hobbling on his crutches as he made his way back over to the couch to sit down after his opening the door for them. He had spent the entire week that he had been out of commission watching movies on the televsion and feeling miserable.

"Damn slim…you look like some shit." Man took a seat next to him.

"Fuck you moe kill. I am not feeling it Man, so don't you come over here with that bullshit!"

"Dee, I understand how you feel, but you can't live all cooped up like this. All the girls have been asking and wondering about you. They want to know if you are good?" Will leaned forward a bit resting his elbows at his knees.

"Here is three-thousand dollars for you." Man pulled the cash from his pocket.

"Why the hell you giving me your money for?" Dee counted the money pulling fifties, twenties and one-hundred dollar bills.

"Me and Will have been on the block covering your graveyard shift for you. A couple of your *Bones* have been looking for you." Man stood up heading into the kitchen.

"Oh yeah, China been around the way with your cousin and them. She been asking about you like crazy." Will grabbed the remote to change the channel on the television.

"Aye man. While you in the kitchen make us a steak and cheese with some fries." Dee yelled out to Man.

"Nigga get your one working foot ass up and make it yourself." Man said laughing out loud.

Dee grabbed one of his crutches hopping quietly into the kitchen.

"Talk that shit now nigga." Dee held the crutch in the air as if he were going to hit Man with it.

They both laughed giving each other some dap.

I missed you slim, but you look like you stink. Go and wash your nasty ass… or… something." Man told him turning his nose up.

All of them burst into laughter at what Man had said knowing that he was telling the truth. Dee had been living foul as hell since his accident. Obliging to his homies requests, he hopped his way into the bathroom to freshen up while they cooked. For the first time since he had broken his ankle Dee felt good and he was laughing thanks to his home boys Will and Man. When Dee finished dressing himself he returned to the living room. Will was rolling up some tree and Man was placing the food they were about to eat onto the table. Dee grabbed his cellphone from its charger so he could begin looking at all the missed calls and text messages that he had. He scrolled through his phone.

"Damn. That girl called and texted me." Dee said out loud not meaning to.

"Who called?" Will asked taking a seat being nosey.

"Why your nosey ass need to know? If you must know, it was that girl I met from a few weeks back when we walked through Adams Morgan." Dee said picking up a French fry from his plate dipping it into the ketchup. "This homemade shit here is on point. Let me find out you all domesticated now and shit." He said joking with Man.

Man held up his middle finger at Dee first, then at Will.

They laughed while their teasing Man about his ability to cook so well. They ate until they were full and ready to get their high on. They returned to the living room. With each of them taking a seat in the room, Will sparked the blunt up. They passed the jay around until it went out. After that they decided to hit the block, so that Dee could show his face letting people know he was okay. When they were inside the car Dee sat in the back seat. He sent MeMe an Asap text:

Hey… I'm sorry for the delay…. but what's good sweetheart?

Hey there stranger. I am in class, but can I call you when I get out?

Of course beautiful. Don't forget.

As anticipated everyone was happy to see Dee. They gave him dap telling him they wanted him to come back to school soon. Some people even signed his cast for him. While he was mingling among friends his phone vibrated.

"Hello."

"Hey there Dee. This is Meme. Just calling to see how you have been?"

"I've been good. I just broke my ankle a couple of weeks ago."

"So sorry to hear that. What you up to today?"

"Well…I'm tryna' see you today if it's not a problem." Dee was hoping that it wasn't.

"Okay. Where are you now?"

"I'm over on Fuller and Mozart now. Not too far from where I first met you."

"Just text the address and I'll be there. I drive a silver Honda. See you soon."

It took Dee no time to text her the address. He was eager to get to know the sexy woman he had booked weeks ago. Twenty minutes had passed by before Dee saw the silver Honda turning left onto Fuller Street. Knowing that it was her he told everybody he would be right back. Will and Man were about to say something to him, but when they saw him going in the direction of the silver Honda with a woman in the driver's seat they knew what was up. Dee hopped into her car giving her direction as to where she could park. It was up the street a little ways. They sat inside the car talking for about fifteen minutes before their getting out and giving each other a hug. After that they sat outside of the car leaning against it while getting to know each other better. They walked for a brief moment so Dee could move his leg while asking questions that they thought might be of importance such as where they were from, how old they were, types of foods they liked, and if they were in a relationship. They even returned to the car and drove away from the block to get ice cream from Ben and Jerry's in Georgetown. While they both had enjoyed the ice cream they enjoyed joking around with each other more. When China drove Dee back on the block to drop him off she promised him they would hook up again despite her having a boyfriend. One would have thought they had known each another for years in the way they had communicated so well together.

Chapter Thirteen

It had been a month since Dee had broken his ankle. Thanksgiving was a few days away. He and his family were on their way to visit with family in Warrenton Virginia. Dee made sure he took a couple of *eight balls of butter* with him because he remembered back in the day his father did major business with his family that lived down in the country selling that crack cocaine that looked like *butter.* If he was to be on point he was about to make some major paper. Yes, his pockets were about to become full with many dollar bills. When they pulled up to his Aunt's house Dee stepped out of the car planting his one good foot on the ground while hobbling to keep his weight off of his injured ankle. His cousin's came rushing to the car to greet him, giving him some dap. They hugged his mother and his grandmother. When all the welcoming had settled down Dee and Fiz went out to the backyard with their big cousin Kenny following along to roll some *Dro* and to catch up on some things. Fiz sat in a chair and started to roll up two *Backwood jays*, while Dee and Kenny walked out to the barn that was located behind the house. Once inside, Dee stood over near the horses petting one while Kenny got straight to the point.

"How has your Pop's been?"

"He is doing pretty well. I will be going out to visit with him this summer when school lets out." Dee shuffled his feet around in some loose hay that rested on the floor of the barn.

"You make sure you tell him for me I said what's up."

"For sure Cuz. I got you."

Kenny looked at him up and then down making a subtle observation of his expensive attire. "So just what are you doing up in the big city? You look like money with those clothes and jewelry you wearing."

Dee laughed looking down at his outfit along with the *ice* he had on. He had to admit that his new swagger did smell of fresh money. He felt taller knowing that people were taking notice. What his cousin thought was an observance had actually been a great compliment. "I have taken over my father's business." He proudly pulled out one of the *eight balls* he had brought along with him to show Kenny.

Kenny's eyes enlarged to the size of quarters. Dee returned the crack rock to his pocket. "Let's head back to the house now with the others before they come out here looking. We'll speak later."

Fiz had already sparked up the jays by the time Dee and Kenny had joined them again. Before they had realized it they were all sitting together in a circle getting high as jets. The temperature dropped and they moved into the house where more family joined them sitting around the table eating, laughing and telling stories that would be heard by Dee for the very first time. There were generations from his mothers' side of the family that Dee had not met before, or had heard from in years. It made him flashback to the possibility of the memories he may have missed out on when his mother had chosen drugs instead of being with him. He had worked hard at his forgiving her, but forgetting it all was a different thing. But on this day he was only going to allow himself to feel the love. Seeing his grandmother there with her peoples having such a great time was heartwarming. It made him smile to a point of his almost crying when he saw her trying to dance to the Electric Slide. His grandma had mad moves even when a few of them ended up going in the wrong way. Later on that same evening after everyone was feeling stuffed from eating the turkey and all the fixings that went along with it, Fiz pulled Dee to the side reminding him how people who lived in the country buy and sell

Butter. Dee thought it would be a perfect time to talk with his cousin Kenny who at the time was hanging out in the kitchen chopping it up with Uncle Earl.

"What's up Dee?"

"Let me holla at you for a moment Cuz."

Dee followed Kenny down the hallway. Kenny opened the door to the stairs that led them down into the basement.

"I got a *meatball?*" Kenny pulled out a hundred dollars.

"One-hundred. Okay, that's cool." Dee handed him two pebbles.

Dee exchanged numbers with his cousins before his leaving, but with only those who were about making the money and not the bullshit.

Chapter Fourteen

Dee had an appointment with his doctor to find out if his ankle was completely healed. He waited in the examining room for his doctor to return with his x-rays. He was happy when the doctor told him the news that he would remove the hard cast and replacing it with a soft one.

"I have looked over the x-ray and your ankle appears to have been healing well. Much faster than expected, which is good news."

"That's great news Doc." Dee grinned.

"We will need to place your leg in an air-soft cast for four weeks. I remind you not to play any ball, and you will need to have a little rehab over at Howard hospital."

Dee pulled his pants on and slid his foot into his shoe. He made a quick stop by the receptionist's desk on his way out to schedule his next follow up appointment. Once he was outside in the hallway he called his boys sharing with them his good news. They made plans to all meet up around the way with one another after school so they could talk about their next move in the game. Neither Will, Dee, nor Man wasted time getting down to business and to the point when they had their meeting. Will spoke first about the good Coke they were getting on the regular. He then continued to speak aboout how much his building was pumped around yellow brick, and also how his cousin from Atlanta was coming to the city to stay for a while. Man went right into saying that his aunt and his cousins on Twenty-first Street Northeast were running the streets, and he was about to move with her to shut the game down and make some major moves with Ant, Lo and Buddie. Dee let them know that he was going to talk with Pun about Uptop as well as to talk to Moe, Larry and Leon about being on the team taking over the Rec for them due to the fact that he had on lock a million dollar town in Virginia with his cousins, and he was going to leave there every other week making pick-ups and drop offs to everybody. They all decided it was time to talk with Fatz, Phil, and Jeezy about the next moves they were going to be making. Dee, Will and Man did not waste any time after the meeting with their going straight to the Rec.

Running into Meek, Moe, and Larry, Man told them how he felt about them being on the team asking if they wanted to make some real money. They were down with the idea, so Will shot them the numbers and told them that they were giving them the ounces for free until they were able to get their money up. Off of every ounce they had to give to Dee, Will, or Man fourteen-hundred dollars when they came for pick-up. They agreed. Dee told them to give him three days to get back at them. Dee took out his phone calling Pun's cell phone. Pun already knew what time it was. They met on Seventeenth and Fuller to talk about the future moves they had planned. Pun told them he was ready to get some real money and that he was tired of dimes and dubs. Will, told him the plan and how things were going to go. Because Pun was alone by himself grinding, they gave him a few of their best customers that had spent fifty dollars, or better every time they showed. Since Dee, Will and Man brought Larry and Meek, onto the team they took the rest of the day spending time to come up with some good numbers and points, so that when they met up with Fatz, he could see the way they were trying to make the world theirs like *Tony Montana*.

<u>Dee</u>

After Will came up with the profit amount that he thought everybody was going to make he called Fatz asking him to meet up. Fatz agreed and they met up on Seventeenth and E Street

Northeast. When Dee and his boys arrived at the place for the meetup with Fatz, he was sitting in the backyard popping bottles and jaw-jacking. When Fatz gave the word that he was ready they followed him inside the house. Each of them sat down on a crate before their getting right to it. They all thought Will's plan made a lot of sense. about how much each of them was going to profit in the next couple of weeks having eighty percent of the city on lock. Fatz looked at them and saw how serious they were telling them that he was down. He even went as far as telling them he was going to inform his *Plug* about the moves they had in mind to make. He also told them he would introduce the *Plug* personally in the event that something happened they would still have a loyal Plug.

Dee

It was Friday and Man decided to call one of the bodyguards that worked at the Heaven and Hell Club over on Eighteenth Street, known as Adams Morgan. He told him he had some extra Loud for him and two-hundred dollars if he would let us inside. The bodyguard gave each of us a stamp on the hand allowing us to enter with no problem.

Here we were in Heaven and Hell ready to turn up. Will, Man, G, Larry, Moe, Leon, Pun, and of course, myself. I did not waste any time stopping the waitress and giving her an order. When she returned she sat fifty shots of Patron onto the top of the table. Before we downed each of the shots I made a toast:

"I want to make a toast to my team G.P.B. *We come as one, and we leave as one.* Uptown **G**et **P**aper **B**oys. After I said that it was on. We took shot after shot. The club had become packed and I swear on my mother that everybody was there. I saw the P5, my cousin and her girls. I even bumped into one of my father's old partners by the name of Sean. He was a good dude and he had never snaked-out my father, not to this day. We exchanged numbers and I told him I would get at him. When the night was over we all went our separate ways. Will was going to drop Man off on Twenty-first and Maryland Avenue before his going home on Fifth North Capital. I walked the way to my grandmother's house. When I arrived there Man's sister Patrice was standing out front talking on her phone. I asked her if she could open the door for me. She put her index finger up in the air asking me to hold on one minute. When she finished talking on her phone she looked me up and down before walking to the door. I was twisted and I had not paid any attention to what she was doing. She opened the door and waited for me to step inside. When we were walking upstairs I grabbed her ass. It was something playful I always did when we were by ourselves. When we made it to the top of the stairs she placed her hand at the back of my neck before grabbing my dick with her other hand.

"If you are not scared, and are ready for me then meet me in the laundry room in ten minutes."

She released me before her walking away and into her apartment as if nothing had happened. My grandmother was sleeping so I kissed her on her forehead before going into my room to get undressed from out of my street clothes. I pulled on a pair of sweatpants and a tank top. I grabbed the half of jay that was in the ashtray before I went down to the basement. No one was there. I I was feeling Patrice had only been joking with me so I sat down in a chair and sparked a jay until I spotted her coming through the laundry room doors with a black night gown on. I threw the jay out the opened window that was slightly opened. I moved towards her grabbing her ass then kissing her soft and passionately. She pulled the tie string to my sweatpants loosening them around my waist so she could pull my boxers down to begin stroking my snake until it became rock hard. She stooped down to the floor on both her knees and she went to work as if her life depended on it. I grabbed at her head, but she kept pushing my hand away. When I felt my body becoming weak I pulled my snake out before I passed out. When she pulled her gown over my head she surprised me with a freshly shaven cat that was crying for her dog to come bite her giving her what she had been waiting for. I made her place her knees in the chair bending her over while I played with her clit and pussy hole at the same time. When I she was moist enough I put a gold pack on and went to work. Even though she was more of a plus size girl I was loving the deep sensation. After about forty-five minutes of my pounding the cat from the back we both came. I then collapsed on her back after every ounce of liquid left my body. That was the beginning of something we would never forget. That week when we went back to school Patrice and her friends kept whispering and giggling every time they saw me. I already knew what that was all about. I just hoped they were not laughing at me, but with me.

Penny

In class I was always sitting by this big butt girl named Penny. After I had broken my ankle she had begun talking to me. I used to catch her looking at me from time to time.

"Dee, you are missing too many days,"

"I know. But right now I have been busy with a lot of things."

"You need to be taking this seriously because when school is finished and you do not have an education it is going to be difficult for you to get a job." she looked him in the eyes.

"I know Penny. I will try to get it together. Do you want to chill and talk more during lunch?"

"I will think about it Dee. I just want you to take school a bit more seriously."

When class was over Penny agreed to meet up with Dee after the next class for lunch. When lunchtime came around Dee shot out of his class and damn near ran to the lunch line so he could be the first student to pay for some wings, pizza and fries. He sat down at the table where he and his boys would sit most of the time. Penny came in and seeing Dee at the table she sat down with him. Dee told her she could have anything she wanted from his plate. Minutes later, Will, Man along with two other girls that Dee had seen around the school sat down with him and Penny. After Dee and Penny had finished eating their lunch they walked together to the vending machine getting snacks. They walked along the hallways talking about future plans and where they saw each of their lives in the next five years. Dee enjoyed Penny's sense of humor and her kindness. He also liked the fact that she cared about his future and well-being in life.

"If you ever need any help just ask me." Penny stood facing Dee showing sincerity on her face.

"Okay Penny, I got you. Say no more."

Chapter Fifteen

Fatz waited no time to set the meeting up with Will, Dee and Man to meet with his Plug. When he called Will to tell him the time and place to meet with him, Will was all ears and knew their plan was going their way for sure now. Will was able to get ahold of Dee, but Man did not answer his phone. After his giving Dee the details on the place and the time, he focused on what he needed to wear. He wanted to appear business sharp. He showered before his putting on clothing that he felt would be appropriate attire for the restaurant they would be meeting in. When they arrived to the restaurant they gave the hostess their names. She immediately escorted them over to a table that sat in the back near a window where Fatz and Jeezy had already been seated. They proceeded in giving one another dap before taking their seats. Fatz informed them that the Plug was on his way there. Dee excused himself to leave heading to the restroom. When he finished using the toilet he washed his hands before taking a quick look at himself in the mirror. While manuevering his way back towards the table he could not believe his eyes. The Plug was his father's old friend Sean. The same Sean he had run into weeks ago at the club Heaven and Hell. Once he was back at the table he gave Sean a handshake telling him it was a pleasure to meet him. They both kept silent that he already knew one another. Placing their order with the waitress for appetizers, wine and then their main courses they began getting down to business. Will began the conversation by pointing out the profits, and how less of a risk it would be if they invested their money in the right manner. Sean sat listening while taking everything Will had said into consideration making a mental note in his head for the future. When their meeting ended Will made sure that he asked for the check. He paid, as well as his leaving a fifty dollar tip for the waitress. To some people what he did was nothing, but to Sean it showed him that Dee was just like his father. Just before Dee was about to get in the car with Will, Sean approached him.

"Aye Dee. Come ride with me. I will drop you off wherever you need to go.

Standing in front of his 320 Benz, Fatz looked at Jeezy wondering what that was all about. Dee gave Will dap. He told him that he would catch up with him sometime later, and for him to drive safely. Dee hopped in the Bentley Fly Spur W12 with Sean taking no time to pull off.

"So this is what you have been up to since your father has been gone."

"No. But it is a long story."

"I'm all ears. I got all day." Sean was serious.

Dee was not sure where he should begin, so he just spoke from anywhere as Sean listened. Dee told him how his mother had become strung out on drugs when his father left the country to flee the law, and that he had been living with his grandmother until she recovered. He told Sean how he had broken his ankle and messed up his dreams of the NBA. He went on to tell him how he had found the crack drug in the alley and he had not looked back since. Dee leaned his head back against the headrest feeling heavy as he heard his own life story moving so quickly.

"I came up with the idea to form the G.P.B. to get the money from all over the DMV."

Sean could sense Dee's emotions once he had finished telling him his story.

"That's some real shit you have been through. I don't know if what I say will make you feel in anyway that's different, but I talk to your father on the phone every day. He is the reason why I am still up in the game.

"What do you mean Sean?" Dee asked searching for more info.

"I am going to be nothing, but up front with you son. Your father is still the Plug, and he has been operating through our shipping company."

When Dee heard that he became saddled in his thoughts. Dee told Sean to drop him off over to his mother's house. He remained silent for the rest of the ride. Sean pulled up to the building let him out making certain that he had Dee's number before his pulling off.

Chapter Sixteen – Major Move

All together Will, Dee and Man had six ounces of *Butters* left from their last batch, so Dee took it to the streets selling it hand to hand. It took them three days before they had cold blooded cash in their hands. They went to Dee's mother's house where they counted each and every dollar bill. After the last bill had been counted the totaling amount was Fifteen thousand one-hundred fifty dollars.

"The next time we do this we need to pay some *butt-naked hoe's* to count all this *cheddar* out." Man wiped the sweat from his forehead.

Dee paid Man's comment no mind. He walked to his closet to retrieve the Hugo Boss duffle bag, which he needed to place the money in. He then called Sean.

 Ring…ring…ring.

Just when Dee was about to hang up a raspy voice answered.

"Hello."

"Hey can I speak to Sean."

"What's up Dee? This Sean."

"My bad for waking you up Sean, but I need to see you when you are not busy."

"Okay Dee. Just give me a couple of hours. I just made it back home from the West Coast. The time change threw my sleep pattern off."

"Okay. Just don't forget. Dee hung up."

"Since we have to wait on Sean, where the damn weed at?" Man asked.

"I got a half of a jay in my ashtray." Dee stood up to get the Backwoods jay.

"That shit ain't going to be enough to get us high." Man told him as he scrolled through his phone to call Jeezy. "Hey Jeezy what's good?" Man asked through his phone.

"Who this?" Jeezy said as he drove up Georgia Avenue.

"This Man- Nigga where you at?"

"I'm on the Avenue fam."

"Well I need to holla at you real quick about a Vick." Man spoke to him in code for the seven grams of Loud.

"Okay. Give me about ten minutes. Meet me in front of the Murray's Shopping Center.

"Will do. Say no moe." Man turned his attention back to Dee and Will. "What ya'll got on this Loud?"

Will and Dee told Man to get a half ounce of Loud while they each pulled out a fifty dollar bill. That would keep them straight for a couple of hours. When Man left the house and when came back inside he had with him an ounce of some new shit called *Green Crack*. Will pulled a pack of Honey Berry Backwoods from his coat pocket. They sat there rotating jay after jay. Before they realized it they had fallen asleep. If it had not been for the loud ringing of Dee's phone they would have missed Sean's returned call. Dee had answered his phone in the nick of time. While on the phone conversation with Sean, Dee let him know that he was at his mother's house. Sean didn't waste any time going to meetup with them. Once Sean was outside Dee walked out with the duffle bag to the car. Dee noticed the Champagne colored 550 Benz parked in the back alley in the cut. It was Sean. He slid inside and onto the seat of the front passenger side giving Sean some dap.

"What's up triple OG?"

"Nothing. Just came back from Cali."

"Cool. I called to give you this." He handed over the duffle bag to Sean. with the fifteen thousand racks inside of it.

Before his giving Sean the opportunity to speak Dee said, "Off bucks... there is fifteen thousand dollars in there."

Sean opened the bag and right there and then he knew Dee was about the paper.

"Look here Dee...This is what I am going to do. I'm going to give you a Bird on the strength of your Pops.' With the money you just gave me I'm going to bless you with twenty ounces. Just make sure next time you don't just give me cash like this. Get a woman on your team. I will give you an address and you let her do the pick-ups and the drop offs. But for the meanwhile, I will get my girl Terry to drop things off to you. Just text me a good place and I will do the rest."

They shared dap just before Sean's pulling off. Step one of Dee's plan was done.

Shit was about to get real and the only woman he could think to run the operation under radar with an iron fist was Niesha, and maybe his homie Tia or his cousin Kesha from time to time. Dee had a lot he needed to think about and he had to think fast. After the word had gotten back to both Will and Man about what Sean had said about them finding a spot, Will knew of the perfect place, so he shot to Sean a quick text message. When Will and his family had been preparing to move away from the hood he had met an old timer. His name was Joe. Joe owned a couple of old warehouses in the DMV. In exchange for some good *Coke* Joe was willing to allow Will to store his belongings there in one of the warehouses. Once Will had moved he still dealt with Joe so he still had a key therefore step two of their plan was checked off of their list. Even though Will no longer dealt with Niesha as he once had been, he still had kept in contact with her. Since his relationship with China the relatonship between him and Neisha was none other than just a good friendship even though there had been some chemistry between them earlier on.

<u>**Dee**</u>

After Dee sent Sean the address to the drop off spot, he had not wasted time calling his cousin Kesha or texting his girl, not girlfriend Niesha. He chose not to say too much while talking over the phone so he asked his cousin to meet him at the mall in Silver Spring. He planned to meet with his cousin first, before his meeting up with Niesha later on in the same mall. When Dee and Kesha met he shared everything with her. Kesha was his older cousin that he shared pretty much all that went on in his life with. They walked around the mall shopping a little before their stopping at the food court to eat burgers and french fries. They talked for hours with Dee filling her in with all the details. Kesha had agreed to being, the available driver for the pick-up and the drop-offs by the end of their conversation. Dee had guaranteed her she would receive significant pay that already had her going to the bank. When Dee met up with Niesha things did not go as smoothly as he had thought they would. In fact, they had gone into an entirely different direction. Neisha was so wrapped up into Dee's swagger, that she did not much care about any potential risks concerning her picking up the money, counting it, or putting it in the safe for him. Her concerned was in getting to know more about why he had never made a move on her so they could get to know one another better. The crazy thing was that even though she and Will had been seeing one another from time to time, they had never had sex. She herself felt that Will was not her type, but it was different for her when she had met Dee. When she was near him her pussy muscles twitched each and every time. Dee had explained everything to her just as he had done earlier with Kesha. His telling her how much money she was going to make after every trip he thought would entice her. He listened to her waiting for her response hoping she was cool with everything, but something in her eyes told him her mind was not fully focused on any of what he had said to her. Little did he know that he would be hit with an element of surprise that would kick him square in his ass. Niesha went straight into it letting the cat out of the bag. After his listening to her rattle on for twenty minutes or so, Dee was left speechless. He had not said a word and that was mainly because Niesha had not stopped her talking long enough that would allow him to get a word in edge wise. He felt as though he had just swallowed a thickness down inside of his throat. Dee could not believe all he had heard that had come out of her mouth. She told him how much she was in love with him. How she and Will had been just good friends. How her relationship with Will was never at risk of becoming serious. After his hearing the long speech that Niesha had given he needed to have a very stiff drink, or a hit as soon as possible. He was becoming totally pissed off with her. And the fact still remained that if she was so into him, why had she been pulling Will along by his nose all this time? This was not the time for him to be side-tracked thinking about the crazy shit Niesha had been talking about, or doing.

"Niesha…just what in the hell are you saying?" Dee waited for her to answer as he glanced at his Movado watch because his time was ticking, and Niesha was wasting most of it.

"Dee, you know I have always had feelings for you, so don't play me like you didn't know."

"Niesha! I don't know what in the hell you are saying. Besides I did not ask you to come here to meet for all this. Right now I am only trying to get paid…not laid."

"What do you mean by that?" *Did he just call me a ho?* "I am trying my best to tell you how I really feel about you. I really want to know how you are feelin' about me." Her voice trembling with both hurt and false hope.

"You know that Will is my boy. How you gonna' stand here asking me to be disloyal to him like that?" Dee had disbelief all over his face.

Dee was trying his best to retain his cool. Niesha was busy going left blowing too much static his way. True they were friends. Good friends he had thought, so why all of a sudden was she trying to cling to him like plastic wrap? He had no interest, spare time nor the patience for this.

"Niesha! All I need to know right now from you is…are you in or out!"

"Nigga' I'm out!" She walked away from him, but not before her giving him her middle finger along with a switch of her ass.

Chapter Seventeen

Will, Fatz and G. were on the block talking shit while shooting a game of dice.

"Come on baby…mama needs a new pair of shoes." Will threw the dice crapping out.

"Don't be mad. Yo' mama ain't worn no shoes since nineteen-twenty." G said laughing loudly before his picking up the dice blowing on them.

"What's up with Sean and Dee? It seems like lately them niggas been chasing a whole lot of paper together." Fatz spits out.

"Look Bro…I ain't trying to hear none of that shit right now. What's understood don't need to be explained." Will huffed.

"But…."

"Don't you ever forget nigga…it is family that makes us related, but loyalty makes us blood." Will reminded him cutting him off.

Fatz's pistol was in the back of his waistband. When he bent to roll the dice again he felt it slipping. He removed it from beneath his shirt placing it onto the ground just far enough away for it not to be in the way of the game. He was about to roll the dice hoping for a five.

"Roll me a five and I am still alive."

They each laughed at his foolishness unaware of the suspicious black Lincoln Continental with tinted windows that had rolled up on them. The windows eased down slowly. Pow…Pow. The loud sounds of the bullets ricocheting off the concrete are heard as Will, G. and Fatz scurry like mice ducking for cover. G. moves swiftly pulling out his Glock Nineteen shattering the rear window of the car as it swerves. Shots ring back striking Fatz in his back twice as he tries to grab for his Glock, which he had left lying on the ground. Pow…Pow…Pow…Pow…Fatz is struck by the fire once again. This time in the chest. His knees buckle and he goes down falling forward. Shots ring out again as G spins around running over to Fatz. Pow…Pow…Pow. His feet leave the ground as he leaps in the air while his both shooting and dodging bullets. His body comes down and it lands forcibly onto the immobile concrete, but he ignores the sting of his injuries as he rolls over onto Fatz covering him. Pow…Pow…Pow… G manages to hit the guy who was sitting in the front seat. The car speeds away leaving multiple skid marks and a massacre of empty shell casings. Sirens could be heard from a distance as the fresh smell of gun smoke arose from the hot black tar on the street.

G immediately turned his attention over to Fatz. Will waited behind the wall where he had hidden to protect himself. He waited until the coast was clear before he came running out.

"What in the fuck was that?" Will's heart was racing from the shock of it all.

"Nah man…we need to know *who the fuck* that was!" G told him straight up.

G raised Fatz's head slightly trying to keep him conscious. Will's fear heightened even more as he looked down at his wounded brother lying on the ground.

"Is it bad?" Will asked about his brother.

"Looks like he took three. He is bleeding pretty badly. We can't stay here with five-o coming."

"We can't just leave him here like this, *G*?"

Knowing they could not be caught on the scene, G listened for the sirens to judge how close they were.

"We can. And we will. They will take care of him if he lives" he said referring to the EMT.

"We will take care of him if he dies…along with those motherfuckers who just creeped up on us."

Want to know what happens to Fatz? Who shot him? Will he die? And what if he does die? Will the G.P.B. choose to retaliate?

Answers to all your questions are coming soon as the upcoming author D. White spins more twists and turns into his saga of three young boys who find their way into money, chaos and manhood. Come along with him on his journey as he takes the G.P.B. to their next level of intrigue. You will definitely be Elevated.

Email: White.de88@gmail.com
Instagram: @funnymac_
Facebook: Denzil White